# WEEGEE'S WORLD

Miles Barth

# WEEGEE'S WORLD

Essays by

Miles Barth

Alain Bergala

Ellen Handy

**A Bulfinch Press Book**

Little, Brown and Company

Boston  New York  Toronto  London

in association with the International Center of Photography, New York

First published by Editions du Seuil, Paris, in conjunction
with the exhibition "Weegee's World: Life, Death, and the
Human Drama," organized by the International Center of
Photography, New York, on view at ICP from November 21,
1997, through February 22, 1998. The exhibition and tour
of "Weegee's World" are sponsored by the National
Endowment for the Arts.

Edited by Miles Barth

Photographs selected by Miles Barth and Gilles Mora

Graphic design by Ernesto Aparicio

Library of Congress Cataloging-in-Publication Data
Weegee, 1899–1968.
    Weegee's world / Weegee : [edited by] Miles Barth ; essays by Miles Barth,
Ellen Handy and Alain Bergala.
        p.   cm
    "First published by Editions du Seuil, Paris, in conjunction with
the exhibition 'Weegee's World' organized by the International Center of
Photography, New York, on view at ICP from November 21, 1997 through
February 22, 1998" — T.p. verso.
    "A Bulfinch Press Book"
    Includes bibliographical references.
    ISBN 0-8212-2375-5
    1. Photojournalism — Exhibitions.  2. Weegee, 1899–1968 — Exhibitions.
I. Barth, Miles. II. International Center of Photography. III. Title.
TR820.W3974  1997
070.4'9'0744436 — dc21                                              97-11990

First published in France by Editions du Seuil, 27, rue Jacob, 75006 Paris

"Weegee and Film Noir" translated by Alexandra Bonfante-Warren

Bulfinch Press is an imprint and trademark of Little, Brown and Company (Inc.)
Published simultaneously in Canada by Little, Brown & Company (Canada) Limited

Printed and bound by Amilcare Pizzi, Italy

# CONTENTS

Photographer unknown. *Portrait of Weegee (Arthur Fellig)*, c. 1956
Inscribed on image : "To all my Subjects, Weegee."

## Acknowledgments

This book is dedicated to Wilma Wilcox, the woman who is most responsible for carrying on the spirit, tradition, and memory of Arthur Fellig, also known as Weegee. In 1976, Wilma was introduced to the International Center of Photography by its founding director, Cornell Capa, who a year later was co-curator of the first museum retrospective of Weegee's photographs. For many years, Wilma entrusted the ICP with administering the reproduction rights to Weegee's photographs. It was through this relationship that Wilma ultimately bequeathed the complete archive of Weegee's personal effects, and his collection of original prints and negatives, to ICP when she passed away in December of 1993. Her donation made many things possible, not the least of which is this publication, and she knew that Weegee's legacy would remain entrusted to the public through the auspices of ICP. Wilma's announcement that ICP was to be the final resting place of Weegee's life's work, made just two months prior to her death, came at a time when she was contemplating another publication. It is my fondest hope that this is a book she would have been most proud of. ICP is also appreciative of the assistance of Andrew L. Deutsch in making the transition of the Weegee Archive and Collection to ICP a smooth one.

It is with the assistance of many colleagues, friends, and associates who knew Weegee, and with the help of many people who did not, that this publication was made possible. First, I would like to thank my friend Gilles Mora, the editor of the series for Editions du Seuil of which this book is a part, for showing early and continued interest in the project. His knowledge of photography and publishing has been an inspiration.

Support for the publication research and preparation was provided by a grant from The Andrew W. Mellon Foundation. For assistance with the organization of the Weegee Archive and Collection after it arrived at ICP, I would like to thank Joanne Seador and Alexia Hughes, whose work was supported by a grant from the New York State Council for the Arts. For additional help with the continuing refinement of the organization of the Weegee Archive, I would like to thank interns Nicole Carnevale, Tracy Schmid, and Birgit Stoll.

I was deeply gratified by the many letters and telephone calls responding to the Author's Query I ran in the New York Times in October of 1995. An enormous amount of valuable and unknown material was gained from these responses. I also want to thank those individuals who allowed me to interview them: Gretchen Berg, Julian A. Belin, Elizabeth Cooke, the Honorable Norman J. Felig, Dr. Philip Felig, George Gilbert, Kingdon Lane, Louis Liotta, Bernard Livingston, John Morrin, Arty Pomerantz, Lawrence R. Racies, Morris Schwartz, Dr. Charles Kavenaugh Warner, and Rae O. Weimer. I would also like to thank Adam Dolgins for allowing me access to Harold Blumenfeld's personal files on Weegee.

In the age of computers, I am grateful to a number of friends and individuals who assisted me in overcoming my technical deficiencies: Robert Ambrose, Jeffrey Hale, Terence Kent, Frank Miller, and Brian Pendergast. I am most especially indebted to Richard Scott, who helped design the database for the Weegee Archive and on several occasions ran to my office when I thought I was lost in cyberspace. I also greatly respect the work of Cathy Peck, who copyedited the texts in this volume.

For her assistance on a variety of projects involving the organization of the Weegee Archive, I would like to thank Julie Moffat, who was especially helpful in putting the Weegee Distortions into proper order. Her work will enable future researchers to access the large body of photographs Weegee created during the last twenty years of his life. Melissa Rachleff, who worked on the cataloguing of the Weegee Archive under a grant from the National Endowment for the Arts, did much more than was required. It was with her help that a great number of the ideas in my text were solidified, and her research on Eastern Europe and the early years of Arthur Fellig was invaluable. My assistant Bob Solywoda has been involved with the Weegee Archive in every aspect from the very beginning. From supervising the packing at 451 West 47th Street, to the unpacking at ICP, he has as thorough an understanding of Weegee's Archive as anyone can have. In addition, Bob helped organize the negatives, prints, and proof-sheet books, making sure that access to this material was always possible. Priscilla Stahle was able to identify names, locations, and dates for many of Weegee's images that had only been documented when they were originally published. Priscilla's findings brought to light changes in the contexts and events associated with many images which had been inadequately documented in Weegee's own publications, as well as those published posthumously.

Additionally I would like to thank my colleague at ICP Ellen Handy and the French film critic Alain Bergala, who have contributed important essays that help evaluate and contextualize Weegee's contribution to the history of photography, cinema, and culture. I am also grateful to have been able to work with the publisher Editions du Seuil and the designer Ernesto Aparicio, who gave this book its special form.

Miles Barth
*Curator, Archives and Collections*
*International Center of Photography, New York*

## Notes on the Photographs

*The photographs in this publication have been arranged into sixteen sections which correspond to the most significant categories in the Weegee Archive at the International Center of Photography.*

*The identifications of the photographs appear in several different formats.*

*When a caption for an image is printed in italics, it has most often been taken from the first source in which the photograph was reproduced or is text from that source describing the event or person in the image. Whenever possible, this was the first choice to identify the image. In cases where the photographs reproduced in this book had never before been published, notes from the Weegee Archive at ICP were used as the primary source material.*

*When the identification appears in quotation marks, this is the title that Weegee assigned to the image or his own words describing the image in one of his own publications. On several occasions, Weegee assigned more than one title, and these appear on two separate lines.*

*The date cited for each image is its first appearance in a publication (newspaper, magazine, or other) at the approximate time the photograph was made. Usually, the dates given here are within the same year in which the photographic negative was made. When no positive confirmation of the date could be found, a circa date is given, preceded by a "c.," which indicates a variance of plus or minus three years.*

*Many of the original negatives in the Weegee Archive and Collection at ICP show signs of serious deterioration due to poor chemical processing or physical damage caused by improper storage or handling. For the reproductions in this publication, every attempt has been made to use Weegee's original negatives, or first-generation copy negatives which he often made for purposes of ease in printing. Several of the copy negatives that Weegee made were from retouched prints, hiding or disguising imperfections in the original negative; in these cases the reproductions which appear in this publication have not been altered further.*

# Weegee's World Miles Barth

*It is seldom that journalism does more than describe what happens, on a purely infor-
mational level and with varying degrees of accuracy. This is as true of journalistic photography as it is of such older forms as writing, drawing or painting. Thousands of photographs, words and drawings are published whose interest, though often very real, is
nevertheless momentary and soon forgotten.*

*We do not remember for long the* what *of events, unless it is accompanied by the*
how *and the* why *in understandable human terms. To give us this, the journalist must
also become an artist, bringing his understanding of life, his sensitivity and, above all, his
own participation in what he is experiencing to a high point of focus, sharpening its
essential reality.* [1]

The photographer Paul Strand wrote these words over fifty years ago, and they
remain as accurate now as when they were written. It was 1945, and the photographer Arthur Fellig, known as Weegee, was at the very zenith of his career. These
words appeared in the New York daily newspaper *PM* on the occasion of the publication entitled *Naked City*,[2] Weegee's most important collection of photographs.

*Naked City* ultimately represented the culmination of Weegee's newspaper photography, dating from his beginning in 1935 as a freelance photographer working
for the New York tabloids, to his association during the first half of the 1940s with
the New York-based *PM Daily*, a newspaper renowned for its graphic design and
photography. The book also served to introduce the persona *Weegee* to a national
audience. In fact, the subtext of *Naked City* was to differentiate the photographer
and the myth through images and text. Weegee's strategy worked. The book immediately captured the imagination of a wide public: here was the real New York
stripped bare of its glamour and sophistication. *Naked City* gave equal weight to
gangs and their activities, to murders, the victims of fire, and the multiethnic
dwellers of tenement living. Weegee's New York was a nocturnal world, where
Bowery bars offered their own particular pleasures, and uptown society was flash-
ing its furs and jewels. Classes and cultures mixed and clashed through the harsh
flash of Weegee's camera.

Weegee ceased working as a photojournalist after 1945, eschewing the rough-
hewn tabloid culture for "art" photography, an approach he followed until his death
in 1968. Nonetheless, scholars, writers, and curators have focused on the ten-year
period represented by *Naked City*, repeating the embellishments, boasts, and the
overall self-aggrandizing theme intrinsic to the text, ultimately perpetuating the
Weegee fantasy for new generations.

Indeed, how Weegee created the *Naked City* photographs is part myth, part legend, and part exaggeration, fabricated by Weegee and others. It is hard to separate
Arthur Fellig, a product of the Lower East Side of Manhattan, from the alter ego,
Weegee, that he carefully concocted. His lack of formal education, the poverty
(almost always present in one form or another through most of his life), and the
competition among the various ethnic groups living on the streets of lower Manhattan gave Arthur Fellig a hardened shell of which Weegee became the bearer. In
the history of photography, few other photographers have created as distinctive
and complex a persona as that of Arthur Fellig.

It is important to begin this investigation, which seeks to separate the man from

1. *"Weegee gives journalism a shot of creative photography,"*
PM Daily, *July 22, 1945 (vol. VI, no. 30, p. 13).*

2. Naked City, *New York: Duell, Sloan, & Pearce/Essential
Books, 1945.*

3. The non-photographic material that makes up the Weegee Archive at the International Center of Photography, New York, contains earlier drafts of the manuscript Weegee by Weegee, unpublished manuscripts for technical manuals, correspondence, address books, and Weegee's clipping collection. However, overall, the material is better on Weegee's post-1950 career as a "creative" photographer. Interviews include family members the Hon. Norman Felig and Dr. Philip Felig. (Weegee's older brother, Elias, changed the spelling of his family's name to Felig.)

4. Lemberg reflects the town's Austrian period when the area was under the Austro-Hungarian empire in the eighteenth century. Prior to that, the town was part of Poland and was known as Lwow. After World War II, in 1945, the town was annexed to the Soviet Union and was known as Lvov. However, because of Lemberg's location near the Russian border, and its history with roots in Polish culture, the town was known alternately as Lwow (Polish), Lvov (Ukrainian), and Lemberg (Austrian).

5. This information comes from one of the few English sources about Lemberg, or Lwow, as it is referred to in the book. The book was written by a Polish nationalist in 1944, during the Nazi occupation. The information is highly biased, and the author is seeking the reinstatement of the Polish monarchy. However, the book does provide an outline of the political and cultural events that took place in Lemberg since the 1300s. See Dr. Stefan Mekarski, A Page of Polish History, Poland: Kolo Lwowian Londyn, 1944, 1991, pp. 35, 68-70. See also Barbara Kirshenblatt-Gimblett's introduction to the 1995 edition of The Culture of the Shtetl (see note 6). Towns in Poland were known for their cultural diversity (Italians, Scots, Armenians, Tatars, Greeks, and Hungarians) and the corporate structure allowed them to do business. "The various native groups (Poles, Lithuanians, Ukrainians, etc.) were land peasants. The groups were divided into neighborhoods ... the central part of town was the business center ..." (p. xix).

6. Irving Howe and Kenneth Libo, How We Lived: A Documentary History of Immigrant Jews in America, 1880-1930, New York: Richard Marek Publishers, 1979, p. 3. See also: Mark Zborowski and Elizabeth Herzog, The Culture of the Shtetl, New York: Schocken Books, 1995, 1952.

7. The first four Fellig children – Elias, Usher, Rachel, and Philip – were born in Europe; the second three Fellig children – Molly, Jack, and Henrietta – were born in New York.

8. Howe and Libo, p. 65.

the myth, by ascertaining in what way the two are linked. As the Strand quote above indicates, the view Weegee offered through his photography is a decidedly singular vision. This essay will consider the way in which Weegee's photographs were part of an autobiographical project. Photography served as an outlet, a mode of coming to terms with the aspects of his life, personality, and influences.

The major research tools used for this text came from the Weegee Archive and Collection, housed at the International Center of Photography in New York. Unfortunately, the primary materials that exist on Weegee's early life are minimal. Most of what is known about his childhood comes from his memoir, Weegee by Weegee, written in 1961, seven years before his death. This memoir, however, provides a decidedly biased view of his youth and early career. Additional information is gleaned from articles published prior to his memoir, interviews with family members, friends, assistants, and colleagues as well as articles about Weegee and the manner in which he worked.[3] To understand him, and the person who had the tenacity to make the images he became most famous for, it is necessary to recount several significant events of his life.

### The Early Years

Usher Fellig (pronounced UU-sher) (later Arthur) was born in 1899 to Rachel and Bernard Fellig, a Jewish couple who lived in the northeastern town of Zlothev, outside the city of Lemberg in the former Austrian province of Galicia, now part of Ukraine.[4] This area was referred to as the Russian Pale of Settlement, an area spreading from the western cities of Russia (from the south near Odessa, moving northward towards Kiev, Minsk, and Riga) throughout Poland, and including the provinces of Galicia (Austria) and Bukovina (Hungary). At the time of Weegee's birth, twenty-nine percent of Lemberg was Jewish. The other sizable minority was Ukrainian, with a native Polish population the majority. As in most Eastern European cities, ethnic minorities lived in particular districts and frequently were not allowed to own land. Thus the native Polish population were the landowners, largely employed in agrarian trades, while the Jews, Ukrainians, and other minorities ran businesses, and leased land from the town's large estates.[5] Although the city was multiethnic, its diverse groups lived separately in demarcated districts. The Jewish district was commonly referred to as the shtetl, where "the central value was learning — biblical and talmudic commentary immersed in moral judgment and intellectual refinements."[6] However, by the nineteenth century, religious Jews coexisted with a growing population of secular, or assimilated, Jews, which resulted in cultural tensions within the Jewish districts.

Usher was the second of seven children.[7] His father was deeply religious, and harbored aspirations of becoming a rabbi. However, to earn a living, the elder Fellig ran a business inherited from his wife's family, supplying food and other provisions to the Austrian army. Most likely Fellig acted as an intermediary between the local farmers and the central government, a typical business occupation for Jews of that period. The success of the Fellig family business was determined by the social and political climate. In nineteenth-century Lemberg, the political winds were constantly shifting. When Lwow, as it was originally known, was ceded from Poland to the Austrian empire in the late eighteenth century, it entered a period of relative tolerance. Under Austrian rule, in 1867, Lemberg adopted its own constitution and was governed by elected officials who were "politically democratic," and boasted a "liberal electoral law."[8]

Photographer unknown. Weegee's parents – Rachel and Bernard Fellig, c.1920s

9. Power shifted between the city's two political parties. The National Democrats (Austrian) were generally more tolerant toward ethnic minorities, and the Polish Socialist Party dominated area politics. The city's strong Polish nationalist spirit sought a return of the Polish monarchy. Student uprisings against Austrian rule at Lemberg's university were a common occurrence during the late nineteenth and early twentieth centuries. Howe and Libo, p. 11. This violence can be seen as a precursor to what befell the Jewish population in the Russian Pale during the rise of the Third Reich. Census data for Lemberg recorded a Jewish population of 135,000. In July 1941 the Nazis invaded and then occupied Lemberg, murdering thousands of its Jewish residents in a violent spree. The Nazis were aided by the Ukrainian population, who shared with the Nazis a deep-seated hatred of the Jews. The city was also the site of the Janowski concentration camp. Today, there is nothing left of the Jewish population that once flourished. See David Kahane, The Lvov Ghetto Diary, Amherst, MA: University of Massachusetts Press, 1990, pp. 5-6.

10. For a general background on Lower East Side conditions during the nineteenth century see Luc Sante, Low Life: Lures & Snares of Old New York, New York: Farrar, Straus, Giroux, 1990.

11. Bernard Fellig eventually received a full-time position as assistant rabbi at a synagogue on Gouverneur Street in 1918.

12. Weegee by Weegee: An Autobiography, New York: Ziff-Davis Publishing Company, 1961.

Around 1905, a change in local government had disastrous results for the Fellig family business. The loss of many Army contracts, most likely because of Fellig's Jewish background, left the family on the brink of ruin. This change in government was also part of a larger anti-Semitic campaign which spread throughout the Russian Pale in 1903. Pogroms, on a scale not seen since the 1880s, were once again perpetrated against the Jews, resulting in a marked influx of Jewish immigration to the United States and England. In 1905, Russian revolutionaries almost succeeded in overthrowing the Czar. The aftermath led many more Jews to flee Eastern Europe.[9]

It was in this context that Fellig lost the family business in Lemberg. Having little money and few prospects for future employment, Bernard Fellig left for the United States in 1906. Like millions before him, he arrived in New York and settled on the Lower East Side, with plans to send for his family after he had earned enough money.

### The New Country

Life in his new country was extremely difficult for the elder Fellig. For the first year, he lived with a succession of relatives and friends. Taking a series of jobs that included renting a pushcart to sell household goods, he finally became a janitor in a tenement on Pitt Street, where he lived for free. Dirt, poverty, overcrowding, resulting in disease and corruption, were common afflictions to the residents of the Lower East Side tenements. With more than 500,000 Jewish immigrants settled in an area that was less than one square mile — from Houston Street to the north, the Bowery to the west and running east to the East River — the streets were so crowded that the rooftops became an alternate mode of travel.[10] In addition to his daytime job, Fellig would also teach young Jewish boys Hebrew in preparation for their bar mitzvahs. He also filled in as a substitute rabbi and cantor in various congregations on the Lower East Side, performing weddings and other ceremonies of the Jewish faith.[11]

By the summer of 1910, Fellig had saved enough money to send for his wife, his three sons, and his daughter. When they arrived at Ellis Island, the immigration officials promptly Americanized the names of the Fellig children, Usher now becoming Arthur. In the first years after arriving in America, the family moved often, living at a number of tenements on the Lower East Side, before finally settling in a cold-water flat on Cherry Street. Weegee recalled in his memoir, "We had three rooms on the fifth floor... there was one hall toilet for four families," the standard layout of the Lower East Side's tenement architecture.

Young Arthur Fellig was enrolled in the local public school in the fall of 1910, and was placed in the class for non-English-speaking children. His struggle to learn English was made more difficult since English was not spoken at home. Yiddish, Russian, Polish, and German were the languages of New York's Jewish ghetto. However, young Fellig eventually made it to the seventh grade, becoming an avid reader and, from what he says in his autobiography, "a good student."[12]

From an early age, Arthur Fellig had a passion for music. In Weegee by Weegee, he describes how he was able to save enough money from his after-school jobs to purchase a secondhand violin, and for a time, tried to teach himself how to play. He became consumed with the instrument, practicing every chance he had, including Saturdays, the day of the Jewish Sabbath, when his father thought he should be spending time studying his religion. Any kind of work on the Sabbath was an affront to God and insulting to young Fellig's observant father. Arthur Fellig's growing assimilation into secular American culture, compounded with his regular contact with other cultures, particularly the Irish and Italian, can be seen as part of a larger cultural transformation for many young immigrants. As immigrant parents struggled to maintain their old customs, their children readily adopted the language and mannerisms of America. This growing difference led to generational chasms resulting in increased familial tensions. For Arthur Fellig and his father, their differences caused an estrangement which was never completely resolved.

The stress was only compounded when Weegee began selling candy after school to help his struggling family. After the birth of three more children, the Fellig household was stretched to the limit, and in 1914, Arthur Fellig left home at the age of fifteen. There were many possible reasons for his departure, but what is known is that by his own choice, Fellig remained distanced from his family, seeing them only on holidays and family occasions.

Fellig was able to support himself through a series of part-time jobs, selling candy to factory workers, working in restaurants, doing almost anything to earn the two dollars a week required to live a meager existence on the Lower East Side. According to his autobiography, when no money could be found, Fellig would wander the streets of New York, both day and night. He found refuge in Pennsylvania Railroad Station on the cold nights of winter, and the benches of Bryant Park were often his summer residence. Sleeping in flophouses when he could afford the 25 cents for a bed, he found unofficial teachers among the bums on the Bowery, the destitute and indigent men he met on the park benches or in the train stations. These various inhabitants of the urban landscape, most beaten and battered by the harshness which New York would deal out, were to become Fellig's friends and compatriots, replacing his real family. As an older, successful photojournalist, Weegee revisited the poverty and squalor of his youth. Although his tone was one of bemused bravado, his photographer's eye revealed that during the last years of the Depression little had changed to help the poor and indigent.

Always curious, Fellig discovered there was magic being performed by an itinerant street photographer who would photograph children sitting on a pony, later selling the images to their parents. The alchemy of the street photographer totally captivated Fellig, and soon he began working as his assistant, processing and delivering the small tintype plates and caring for the photographer's pony (often using the stable as his own residence). Eventually, he left the photographer and rented his own pony to continue this line of work.

In 1917, he was hired by the Ducket & Adler Photo Studio at 60 Grand Street. At this studio, which made photographs of objects for traveling salesmen's portfolios and architectural views of many of the buildings being built in lower Manhattan, Fellig was originally hired to sweep floors, assist when and where needed, and run errands.[13] His inquisitiveness and ability to learn in a hurry brought him an early promotion to an assistant to the cameramen, loading and changing the glass plate holders, lugging huge $8 \times 10$ inch and $11 \times 14$ inch cameras, and preparing the magnesium flash powder. Fellig kept the job at Ducket & Adler until he became convinced that he was underpaid for his services. When he confronted his employer, the ensuing argument over wages cost him his job.

At this juncture, Fellig decided to try tintype portraits once again. He purchased a secondhand $5 \times 7$ inch view camera and rented a pony. Fellig would roam the streets on Saturdays and Sundays seeking children to take their photographs. "No

13. From a press release written by John V. Smith at Weegee's request after Weegee's return to New York from Hollywood in 1952.

use shooting on weekdays; the kids were shabbily dressed, and in school," Weegee stated, revealing his attuned business sense.[14] During the week Weegee developed and printed the photographs and went to the children's homes to sell them. As Weegee recalled: "The people loved their children and, no matter how poor they might be, they managed to dig up the money for my pictures. I would finish the photographs on the contrastiest paper I could get in order to give the kids nice, white, chalky faces. My customers, who were Italian, Polish, or Jewish, liked their pictures dead-white."[15]

Fascinating here is the observation of skin tone. The immigrants wanted their children to appear fully assimilated in American culture and, as such, wanted them to appear "white." This clearly demonstrates how the new arrivals to the United States did not automatically perceive themselves as Caucasian, and further, how the racist attitudes of the American culture were rapidly passed through the new immigrant population. The high-key tones of the photograph would be another element that would distinguish Fellig's work as a photojournalist. Although this was to be young Fellig's first independent job in photography, an extended period of bad weather and a misunderstanding with the stable owner put Fellig out of the pony photo business.

It was 1921, and Fellig continued to live on the Bowery, staying in a succession of flophouses and boarding rooms, while frequenting park benches and train stations. He continued to study the violin. "My fiddle became almost as important a part of my life and dreams as my photography."[16] In exchange for his help in making bathroom gin for a musician, he received free violin lessons. Through this same connection, he eventually got a job at a silent movie theater on Third Avenue that consisted of various tasks as well as filling in on his violin to accompany the silent films. One of the most revealing statements that he made in his autobiography comes from this period. Fellig wrote: "I loved playing on the emotions of the audience as they watched the silent movies. I could move them to either happiness or sorrow. I had all the standard selections for any situation. I suppose that my fiddle-playing was a subconscious kind of training for my future in photography."[17]

### The Creation of Weegee

According to his autobiography, Fellig was an avid reader of books, magazines, and the daily newspapers, always keeping a close eye on the help wanted section. After noticing an ad for a part-time position in the darkrooms of the *New York Times,* Fellig was soon drying prints for both the *Times* and their syndication service Wide World Photos. His job consisted of removing the excess water from the prints subsequent to placement on chrome-plated brass sheets that were then inserted into heated dryers in order to produce a high-gloss surface to increase contrast for the engraver. The work Fellig did required the use of a squeegee to remove the surplus moisture: the printers would call out "squeegee" whenever a print was to be prepared for drying. Fellig had never heard of this tool before but was soon proficient enough to be considered by his colleagues one of the most skilled at this task. There are varying versions of how Arthur Fellig acquired the moniker Weegee. Morris Schwartz, a printer in the darkrooms of the *New York Times* from 1921 until 1926, remembers calling Fellig "squeegee boy," which later transmogrified to Weegee.[18]

More importantly, Fellig's position at the *Times* was his first direct contact with the news business. The inside workings of a daily newspaper — how editors select-

14. Weegee by Weegee, p. 17.

15. Ibid., p. 18.

16. Ibid., p. 27.

17. Ibid., p. 27.

18. Author's telephone interview of November 24, 1996, and letter from Morris Schwartz, December 4, 1996.

19. "Weegee: Alias Arthur Fellig" by Harold Blumenfeld, Photographic Business and Product News, February 1969, p. 22.

20. Ibid., p. 23.

21. "The Inside Workings of a National News Photo Service," by Gray Strider, Popular Photography, July 1937, pp. 16, 17, 80, and 81.

22. Weegee by Weegee, p. 28.

23. "Weegee: Alias Arthur Fellig," p. 24.

ed stories to compel their readers, how photographs were cropped and retouched if necessary — was to captivate him for the rest of his life. But common to his employment history, the job at the *Times* was short-lived.

The actual date when Fellig began at Acme Newspictures, his next position, is in dispute. Fellig recalls it as 1924, but Harold Blumenfeld, an editor at Acme who hired him as a darkroom printer, remembers it as 1927.[19] Acme became Fellig's second home, both figuratively and practically. Blumenfeld recalls Fellig was somewhat inept when first hired, but: "He learned fast. In a short time he became one of the best darkroom printers I have known, not just making one salon type print, but turning out more than a thousand prints a day, from negatives calling for a half dozen prints to large runs to a hundred. He was a master craftsman in the darkroom and showed early imagination and trickery by making wonderful double and triple exposures to create what then were his earliest fantasies."[20]

Acme was a source of photographs for three of the major New York dailies, the *Daily News*, the *World Telegram*, and the *Herald Tribune,* and syndicate for photographs and news stories to several hundred other newspapers across the United States.[21] Fellig was kept busy developing negatives and making prints of the photographers Acme employed in New York and around the country. "Over the developing trays in the darkroom at Acme, history passed through my hands," Weegee wrote. "Fires, explosions, railroad wrecks, ship collisions, prohibition gang wars, murders, kings, presidents, everybody famous and everything exciting that turned up in the Twenties."[22]

Acme employed editors who would select the stories of importance, thirty full-time photographers, darkroom technicians, retouchers (for both negatives and prints), and caption writers. The offices were always lively, and Fellig felt that he was a part of a family. When he could not afford housing, sometimes losing his pay in a card or crap game held just after the paychecks were distributed, Weegee would sleep in the darkroom or any vacant office at Acme. He was well liked, and often worked extra shifts when employees called in sick. Fellig was always generous, sometimes to a fault. When he was asked for a loan by one of his colleagues (most of whom were making far more than he was), he never hesitated to reach for his wallet.[23]

At Acme, two additional stories surface on the genesis of Weegee. The first, told by Blumenfeld, states that when the printers at Acme learned that he was a former "squeegee boy" at the *New York Times*, there was constant taunting. But since he had graduated from the print washing area to the darkroom, they began to call him "Mr. Squeegee, " later transliterated into Weegee. The story is different among the agencies' photographers and editors. Within the staff room at Acme, besides the battered decks of cards and the stacks of newspapers from around the country, the craze for the Ouija board was raging. A game that was said to predict the outcome of future events, it used a small plastic device that moved around the board by the so-called "vibrations" of the participants' hands placed on a planchette. The board itself was elaborately designed, incorporating an alphabet to explain words that could give key messages and illustrated with various fictional characters around its border. The story is told that Fellig, with his lack of regard for proper personal hygiene, in the habit of not shaving very often and sleeping in his clothes, looked very much like one of the devilish figures on the Ouija board. Somehow the name stuck, and Fellig (who pronounced it Wee-chee because of his New York accent) would say the origin of the name came from his own clairvoyant powers akin to

Photographer unknown. *Weegee playing poker at Acme Newspictures,* c. 1927

the board's, but the spelling was purely his own.[24] All three stories have credible elements, but it was not until his work appeared on the pages of *PM* that the name Weegee supplanted Fellig.

From time to time, when other photographers were not available, or during the overnight shift to which the newly named Weegee was assigned in the early 1930s, he was asked to fill in and either accompany a photographer to rush the negatives back to the darkroom, or on occasion to take the photographs himself. Having developed so many negatives and prints, he believed that he was fully capable of becoming the star photographer at Acme if only given the chance. Weegee learned many of the tricks of the press photographer's trade in a hurry, shutting down his lens aperture to *f*16, setting the speed of the exposure to 1/200 of a second, and standing ten feet from the subject in his lens; all of this to capture the maximum of tonality, magnify sharpness, stop any unnecessary motion, and be ready to respond in a hurry. Still other techniques he invented or adapted from accepted practices, always carrying additional film and flashbulbs, and on occasion, using flash powder to cover a large fire or rescue scene when the distance at which he was made to stand was too far for any flashbulb to cover the event. Weegee's experience in the darkroom served him well, as the extremely thin negatives of his night photography were not easy to print. Once he made an excellent print from a difficult negative, he would copy it onto fine-grain film, allowing him to make numerous prints of almost original quality in a hurry.[25]

More often than not, the assignments Weegee was asked to cover were the late-night arrests, bookings at police headquarters, fires, auto accidents, and rescues in the midtown area. There was always an early-morning market for photographs from these types of events, and Acme became well known in the trade as being able to supply them.

Acme, like so many of the other syndicates and newspapers, maintained several rooms in what were known as the "shacks" behind police headquarters on Center Market Place, where reporters could sleep, read, or do almost anything else while

24. *Fellig was fascinated with the English language, although he had never mastered proper grammatical skills. Weegee was thus his phonetic spelling of Oujia.*

25. *A number of the negatives in the Weegee Archive at ICP are these copy negatives. The originals in most cases also exist, but many of these are in poor condition and no longer usable.*

they waited for something to happen. They would monitor the shortwave police
radios installed in their rooms or the Teletype machine in the lobby of police headquarters. It was as if the reporters and photographers were vultures, waiting for
their next victim to appear. Weegee, always trying to ingratiate himself with anyone
who could do him a favor, began spending all his spare time in the shacks. Eventually, in 1934, he rented a one-room apartment at 5 Center Market Place, where he
lived (for the most part) until 1947.

In the little time he had off from his responsibilities at Acme, Weegee was now
taking his own photographs. Acme didn't care, as long as they were given first
option to Weegee's night catches. When Acme would not buy or distribute the self-
assigned images he was making, he would quietly peddle them to another newspaper or syndicate. When Acme did buy a photo from him for the New York dailies,
or distribute it nationally, it appeared with the credit line "Acme Newspicture
Photo." This became increasingly disconcerting to Weegee; not having his name
appear on photographs meant that any one of the hundreds of press photographers working for the dailies or syndicates could have made *his* image. Several rep-
etitious discussions on this subject took place with the editors and director of
Acme; however, none yielded any satisfactory results for Weegee.

By late 1935, Weegee had become increasingly restless, wanting to get out on
his own. He realized that it was possible, by taking his own photographs, making
the rounds to the various photo editors at the New York newspapers and news
syndication services, hustling all the time, to be his own boss.

Weegee's success as a freelance news photographer came early. He knew from
his days with Acme that very few of the New York dailies kept staff photographers
on a night shift. His reputation spread quickly for always being one of the first to
arrive at a murder, arrest, fire, rescue, or almost any other newsworthy event
between the hours of 10:00 p.m. and 5:00 a.m. He became so successful in a profession that had so few photographers who were not attached to one of the newspapers or syndicates, that both *LIFE* and *Popular Photography* magazines took notice

and produced profile pieces on him as early as April and December of 1937, respectively. He described his routine, carefully noting his powers of premonition, as follows: "I would drop into Police Headquarters at around 7:00 p.m. If nothing's stirring and my elbow don't itch — and that's not a gag, it really does itch when something is going to happen — I go on back to my room across from Police Headquarters and go to sleep. At the head of my bed I have a hook-in with the police alarms and fire gongs so that if anything happens while I'm asleep, I'm notified… When I get my pictures I hurry back to Headquarters. There is always a follow-up slip on an accident (or crime) with all the names and details coming in over the teletype. I find out who were injured, where they lived, and on what charges they have been arrested, so that I can caption my pictures correctly. Next I go back to my darkroom and develop my prints. By this time it is around six in the morning and I start out to sell my prints."[26]

Although Weegee makes his routine sound simple, it eventually became laborious and taxing.

His contacts inside the police and fire departments, and his friendships with barkeepers, restaurant and nightclub owners, ambulance dispatchers, and street-corner stool pigeons, allowed him to develop an information network that could always lead him to a story if the Teletype machine went dead. Many in the press corps resented his original, and sometimes brash, tactics, pushing past police lines with dubious identification, using disguises, and often paying off informants for information that might lead him to another photograph. But if Weegee did not sell his photos, it meant that he might be back on a park bench, borrowing money for film or hocking his camera for his next meal, something he often contemplated.

In 1938, he became one of the first civilians, and the first *photographer,* to be granted a permit to install and operate a shortwave radio capable of receiving all police and fire transmissions from his car. He was now truly mobile, adding this new capability to his growing arsenal of photo weaponry. He must have felt that more than ever the similarities between himself and his namesake board game were true. From the tenements of the Lower East Side to the whorehouses of the Upper West Side, he was able to cover the entire city.

Few photographers of his generation could keep up with his pace or stamina for the night-after-night photographs of corpses — in the jargon of the newsroom, "roasts" (victims of fires), "dry divers" (people jumping off buildings), or "bottom feeders" (victims of drowning). Covering four to six separate stories in one night, he was relentless and sometimes ruthless when it came to getting his photographs, often making over one hundred dollars a week, which, during the last years of the Great Depression, was considerable.

Weegee was famous for his regular visits to the many haunts he inhabited in the early hours of the morning or on a rare day off. He thrived on the excitement of taking and selling his last photograph, and he loved people and enjoyed conversations with friends or whoever would listen to his latest escapade photographing the underside of New York. As much as Weegee was known for always having a cigar in his mouth and several more in his coat pocket, the battered Speed Graphic camera in his hand, and a camera bag in the same or worse condition, he was never without a good story.

Of the places he would frequent, either for a free meal, cheap drink, hot tip, or just plain conversation, Sammy's was his favorite. Sammy Fuchs opened his establishment in 1934 at 267 Bowery in lower Manhattan. Shortly after it opened,

26. *"Free-Lance Cameraman,"* by Rosa Reilly, Popular Photography, *December 1937, pp. 21-23, 76-79.*

Weegee became a fixture, and whenever he would be absent for several days, Sammy would usually call police headquarters to make sure his friend was chasing a lead on a story. Sammy took out a cabaret license, hired some former vaudevillians, advertised it as the "Stork Club of the Bowery," and changed the name to Sammy's Bowery Follies. The uptown clientele began to appear, attracted less by the entertainers than by the general spectacle of dirt and degradation offered by the neighborhood regulars. On stage, there was always a rousing song being sung, a fake striptease, or a chorus line made up of men and women over the age of sixty, kicking their legs as they probably had forty years earlier. "The Stroll" would take place twice a night. Dora Pelletier, Mabel Sidney, Norma Devine (Sammy's "Mae West"), and a host of other performers would stroll through the aisles purposely to pick up tips.[27]

Sammy's was the scene of many of Weegee's most lighthearted and humanistic photographs, a great contrast to what was taking place on the street or curb just outside the front door. The "poor man's Stork Club" became a refuge for Weegee, a safe haven allowing him to escape the blood and guts that his more salable photographs contained.

It has been written of Weegee that he had little knowledge of his contemporary photographers, only commenting on occasion about Lewis Hine's photographs of impoverished children, calling Alfred Stieglitz "another great photographer," and referring to Pat Rich, a staff photographer for the *Police Gazette,* by saying, "This is my favorite magazine." Few references are made in any of his books or his personal papers to other photographers he knew or appreciated. However, this is not true as it related to the time he spent at the Photo League during the late 1930s and early 1940s. Louis Stettner, a close friend and colleague of Weegee's, described the Photo League: "Born out of the rich and varied political ferment of the twenties and early thirties, the League was, above all, the first progressive, left-wing photography organization in the United States." They would accomplish their objectives, Stettner went on to say, "first, through activities, exhibitions, school lectures and publications of *Photo Notes,* the development and encouragement of photography as a fine art; second, the use of photography as a tool to help working people in their struggles, and to document and interpret their daily lives." [28]

Weegee was not a dues-paying member of the Photo League. However, he frequently appeared and gave impromptu lectures and slide projections, and participated as a judge in contests and other competitions run by the League.[29] He was given his first one-person exhibition there in 1941, entitled "Murder Is My Business,"[30] an honor he never forgot. Weegee was received with great admiration by

27. *"Sammy's Bowery Follies: Bums and Swells Mingle At Low-Down New York Cabaret,"* LIFE, December 4, 1944, pp. 57-60.

28. Allene Talmey, Weegee, Aperture History of Photography Series, Millerton, NY: Aperture, 1978, p. 8. Famous Photographers Tell How, New York: Candid Recordings, 1958 (33-1/3 rpm, long-playing record). Naked City, p. 237.

29. Interview by the author with George Gilbert, September 26, 1996.

30. Weegee had two solo exhibitions in the Photo League clubroom at 31 East 21st Street. Both were titled "Murder Is My Business"; the first took place in August and was immediately followed by the second in September of 1941.

most of the membership, although there were those at the League who felt that his photographs were insensitive to the victims in the images and that he was opportunistic, lacking any social conscience.

The League nurtured and exhibited many important photographers from that period. Weegee was well aware of the work and philosophy of many of them, including Berenice Abbott, Morris Engel, Sid Grossman, Lewis Hine, Arthur Leipzig, Sol Libsohn, Lisette Model, Ruth Orkin, Walter Rosenblum, Aaron Siskind, W. Eugene Smith, and Dan Weiner, as well as many non-American photographers such as Manuel Alvarez Bravo, Henri Cartier-Bresson, Brassaï, and Robert Doisneau. Weegee's participation in many of the League's functions, as well as his frequent visits to the clubroom as one of his regular hangouts, certainly put him in contact with many of his contemporaries.

In June of 1940, a new daily newspaper made its appearance on the stands of New York. It was called simply *PM Daily* and was created by Ralph Ingersoll, with financial support from Marshall Field, the Chicago department store owner. A seasoned editor, Ingersoll had previously worked for the *New Yorker*, *Fortune*, *LIFE*, and *Time*, and he assembled for *PM* a staff of the best and brightest columnists, graphic designers, illustrators, and photographers, producing one of the most lively newspapers in New York City history. A distinct feature of *PM* was its high reproduction value. Ingersoll's background in the magazine world led him to adapt many of the new printing technologies to the tabloid. *PM* was printed using the "hot ink" process, in which hot ink was applied to water-cooled paper, the resulting quality equivalent to a magazine. The words of the paper's first managing editor, John P.

Photographer unknown. *Weegee at his typewriter in the trunk of his 1938 'Chevy,'* c. 1943

Lewis, when he responded to a reader's letter asking why *PM*'s price was almost twice that of any of the other New York dailies, best describe the aims and objectives of *PM*: "The price of *PM* on the newsstands is more deeply tied up with the kind of paper *PM* is than in the case of any other paper about which I know. *PM* was started on June 18, 1940 as an experiment in journalism to see if independent journalists, operating without [any] restriction but the limits of their own consciences, could do a better job of getting to the truth about the news. To guarantee this freedom to the men who put out the paper, it was decided at that time that *PM* would sell no advertising, but would depend for its income only on the man or woman who bought it at the corner newsstand" (August 14, 1940).

Even before the first issue of *PM* appeared, Weegee was offered a position by Ingersoll as a special contributing photographer, but not an official member of *PM*'s staff; Ingersoll knew that Weegee would never accept the offer otherwise.[31] Weegee was allowed to review the daily assignment sheets and select any story that needed to be illustrated, hang around police headquarters and do anything that came in over the Teletype, or just roam the city streets in his police-radio-outfitted auto. Weegee chose to do all three. The only concession asked of him was that he show whatever he did to *PM* before any of the other New York dailies, or any of the weekly newsmagazines. In return for his agreement to *PM*'s offer, Weegee would be paid for each photo that *PM* purchased, published or not, and receive a weekly stipend. Most important, every published photograph would carry a credit that read "*PM* Photo by Weegee."[32] In addition to the freedom of photographing whatever he wanted, Weegee wrote his own captions, and on several occasions, also wrote the stories that accompanied them.

This was as close as Weegee ever got to being on the staff of any newspaper. For the next four and a half years, some of the most important photographs Weegee made during his career were published in the pages of *PM*.[33] Along with the photographs of murders, arrests, fires, rescues, and automobile accidents he was by this time already famous for, he produced story after story within the category of "human interest." These were photographs of what people did for enjoyment during the cold winters and hot summers in the City, photographs of bathing beauty contests or of women's skirts being blown above their heads by gusts from the subway gratings. Weegee also made photographs of children in foundling homes so that missing parents could identify and claim their children, and of the lines of cars waiting for gas during the rationing periods of World War II.

For the first few months, Weegee worked alongside well-known writers who were consultants to the paper, including Dashiell Hammett, Donald Ogden Stewart, Dorothy Parker, Haywood Broun, and Lillian Hellman. Also associated with *PM* were the journalists Erskine Caldwell, I. F. Stone, Frank Hewlett, Max Lerner, Theodore Seuss Geisel (Dr. Seuss), and correspondent Ernest Hemingway, as well as a number of important photographers, including Margaret Bourke-White, John DeBiase, David Eisendrath, Morris Engel, Morris Gordon, Irving Haberman, Leo Lieb, Helen Levitt, and Mary Morris.

Weegee's first published photograph for *PM* was on Wednesday, June 19, 1940, the day after the first edition appeared. It was, by all standards, a typical Weegee image, a "crushed-eggshell wreck of an automobile which crashed into an abutment at Henry Hudson Parkway and 72nd St."[34] *PM*'s concern for the improvement of New York and its citizens is apparent in the following sentence of the same caption. "*PM* hears that there has been persistent agitation to correct this dangerous

31. Author's interview with Rae Weimer, December 21, 1995. Mr. Weimer was an associate editor at *PM*.

32. Weegee's published photographs in the New York dailies prior to 1940 were usually printed without a credit line, or with one of the following credits: "Photo by A. Fellig," "Fellig Foto," or "Credit Arthur Fellig." Prior to this time, the name "Weegee" was rarely published with his photographs.

33. Unlike many of his contemporaries, Weegee did not keep clipping books of his published works. There are many examples of his published images in his Archive at ICP, and a complete list has been compiled of all the work he had published in *PM*.

34. PM, Wednesday, June 19, 1940.

curve, responsible for many accidents; will try to find out if anything is being done to eliminate the hazard." Many of *PM*'s stories were filled with this "will try to find out," or "something should be done" proclamation to correct this or that.

The summer of 1940, when *PM* made its debut, was unusually hot. Weegee was asked to make a series of photographs showing how New Yorkers were surviving the record temperatures. The result was one of Weegee's most remembered and reproduced photographs, the throngs of people at Coney Island published with the headline, "Crowd at Coney Island…Temperature 89…They Came Early, Stayed Late." Below this was a subtext which read, "Cameraman Reports On Lost Kids, Parking Troubles." Weegee was the cameraman and also wrote the text. In it he talks like a reporter, giving the background, and always referring back to himself, writing, "Saturday was very hot. So I figured Sunday ought to be a good day to make crowd shots at Coney Island. I arrived at the beach at Coney Island at 4 a.m., Sunday. The beach was crowded mostly with young couples lying on the beach covered with blankets. I took pictures of them. When I asked them their names they all said, 'It's just me and the wife,' as they pointed to the girl on the sand. I went back to the city."[35] In a similar crowd image that appears on page 24, the caption shows just how much Weegee was after the people side of the story. "The masked man said he was a laundry man, but would only be photographed incognito. The mask is a gag of his; he calls himself the Spider, and likes to frighten people." In a slightly sarcastic tone, the item remarked that "Weegee didn't get the names and addresses of the others in the photo, either," obviously an impossible task considering the hundreds of people in the photograph.[36] Weegee made many photographs of Coney Island, and when they appeared in *PM*, it was almost as if summer had truly arrived: the first lost child, lifeguards performing rescue rehearsals, couples in the sand both day and night, and his ever-favorite crowd shots.

Public holidays were an important opportunity for *PM* to run stories and photographs that celebrated the activities of the common man and woman. Weegee was asked to produce stories of parades, rallies, and public events, whether or not they were associated with the holidays, as it made for good people photographs, which were fast becoming his specialty. For the four and a half years during which Weegee's photographs were a regular part of *PM*, the Thanksgiving issue always carried his images of preparations for the Macy's parade and the men who were given free hot turkey meals in the missions on the Bowery.

But it was his crime photographs that got Weegee the position at *PM*, and it was *PM* that published his best. The example on page 105, which Weegee later retitled "End of a Joy Ride," was actually published with the *PM* caption "Car Crash Upper Fifth Ave., 4 a.m.: The street lights were turned out…two cars crashed. A badly cut-up youngster asks for a cigaret [sic] until the ambulance arrives." Weegee positioned himself just outside the front seat passenger's window and took the photograph of the injured boy being comforted with a cigarette from his friend who was driving. The photograph contains the classic elements of a Weegee image: the central focus of the image contains the boy with his eyes closed, and we can see his reflection in the vent window, a reiteration of the event, and the glowing eyes of a spectator on the opposite side of the car, with others there as well. Weegee went on to say in the caption he wrote for *PM*, "Cops resent accidents that happen around quitting time. Making out reports means overtime, no pay." [37]

Another photograph offers a glimpse into Weegee's loose approach to fact. In what can only be termed his technique of "recaptioning," Weegee used a different

35. PM, *Monday, July 22, 1940, pp. 16-17.*

36. PM, *Saturday, July 5, 1942, p. 7.*

37. PM, *July 13, 1941, pp. 62-63.*

38. PM, *December 28, 1942, p. 7.*

caption for the image when it appeared in *Naked City*, in contrast to what had previously been published in *PM*,[38] illustrated here on pages 114-115. In a dramatic sequence of photos Weegee made as part of a series "Christmas on the Bowery," the first photograph was typical — a bum on the street. As Weegee turned and walked away, about one block later, the man was hit by a taxi, and Weegee returned to photograph the aftermath of the event. Father Joseph L. Melody, a priest from the Holy Name Mission on the Bowery, arrived to administer last rites of the Church. Weegee wants us to believe from *Naked City* that the man, having been given his last rites, will soon die. However, Frank Birskowsky, the man who was run over, is eventually taken to Bellevue Hospital, where he "is expected to recover," *PM* reported.

Possibly his most complex and successful crime photo appeared in *PM* on October 9, 1941, seen here on page 64. It was not often that Weegee ventured to Brooklyn other than to visit the offices of *PM*. However, at 3:15 p.m., on October 8, the children from P.S. 143 in the Williamsburg section of Brooklyn were leaving school when a minor figure in the underworld was slain in his car just outside the school. The gunman ran through the crowd of children, making it impossible for the police who arrived on the scene to try to stop him by using their guns. In one of those coincidences which marked his career, Weegee arrived at the same time as the dead man's aunt, and his photograph catches the horror on her face, the confusion of the children, and the wild scramble of activity, including the aunt's own son tugging at the girl in front of him as he tries to get a look at his dead cousin. At first viewing, the figures look as if they are jumping or being forced towards Weegee's lens. Faces turn in every direction, the hot light of Weegee's flash bounces off their skin, and the city's delicate outline is seen in the background. All these elements, combined with the knowledge that a body lay at Weegee's feet, made this one of the most shocking news photos published in its time. When it appeared in *PM* the next day, it covered the top half of the page, with another pho-

Opposite: *Coney Island at noon Saturday, July 5th, 1942*

*Lovers After Dark, Coney Island*, c. 1943

25

tograph by Weegee — of the dead man's body, already draped with newspaper, waiting for the morgue van to arrive — occupying one-quarter of the same page. (A book review took up the remaining space.)

Weegee was also known for getting the tight close-ups of the arrested criminals at many police precincts where his friends were police officers. The image on page 87 is a good example. The woman, Irma Twiss Epstein, a 32-year-old nurse, has just been arrested for killing a baby in her charge with an overdose of a drug. She told the police that the baby's crying "drove me crazy."[39] In *PM*, the image appeared full page, with a second one printed much smaller of the same woman taken from a farther distance, sitting in a chair and covering her face. Weegee was able to capture criminals with an intimacy that had been rare in newspaper photography, a frozen moment, a curious mixture of calm, distress, and pain.

Weegee's years at *PM* (1940-1945) paralleled World War II. *PM* printed photographs of the war on a daily basis, both syndicated photos from the wire services of the battles and related events, and photos depicting the wartime efforts taking place in New York and around the country. There were many events to cover, from the metal and rubber scrap drives, to the rallies in Times Square and parades to celebrate various victories, and eventually the end of the war. Weegee and the staff photographers at *PM* were constantly involved with covering one or several of these events on a daily basis. Weegee's best-known photographs of these events are the rallies in Times Square at the end of the war in both Europe and Japan, and the welcoming-home parties for GIs in Little Italy and Chinatown.

### "The Critic"

Probably Weegee's most famous image, and certainly his most widely published, was taken for *PM* but never appeared there. The opening night of the Metropolitan Opera in 1943 was advertised as a Diamond Jubilee to celebrate the 60th anniversary of the company. The featured performance was to be a tribute to the U.S.S.R, the Russian opera *Boris Godunov*. In a recent interview, Louie Liotta, a photographer who acted as Weegee's assistant, recalled that Weegee had been planning this photograph for a while. Liotta, at Weegee's request, picked up one of the regular women customers at Sammy's on the Bowery at about 6:30 p.m. With a sufficient amount of cheap wine for the woman, they proceeded to the opera house. When they arrived, the limousines owned by the members of high society were just beginning to discharge their passengers. Weegee asked Liotta to hold the now intoxicated woman near the curb as he stood about twenty feet away from the front doors of the opera house. With a signal worked out in advance, Weegee gave the sign to Liotta, who released the woman, hoping all the while that she could keep her balance long enough for Weegee to expose several plates. The moment had finally arrived: Mrs. George Washington Kavenaugh and Lady Decies were spotted getting out of a limousine. Both women were generous benefactors to numerous cultural institutions in New York and Philadelphia, and Weegee knew that they were well known to every newspaper in New York. Liotta recalled the moment he released the disheveled woman: "It was like an explosion. I thought I went blind from the three or four flash exposures which Weegee made within a very few seconds."[40] *PM* paid Weegee five dollars for the photograph but did not publish it, since the editorial board thought it was not appropriate to show such lavish jewels and furs during wartime. Weegee had also sold the out-of-town distribution rights to Acme Newspictures, which circulated it with the caption, "She is aghast at the

39. PM, *Monday, February 9, 1942, p. 3.*

40. *From an interview with Louie Liotta, December 5, 1996. Mr. Liotta's father worked at Acme in the late 1920s and often brought his son to Acme to interest him in the engraver's trade. Instead, he decided to make photography his career, and would often assist Weegee in the late 1930s and when he was on leave from military service during World War II. He was the assistant to Weegee the evening of November 22, 1943, when this photograph was made. The story Liotta tells is considerably different from the one Weegee tells in either* Naked City, *or* Weegee by Weegee.

41. "Weegee: Alias Arthur Fellig," p. 23.

42. First described to the author by Robert Fowler in a letter
dated October 21, 1995, and confirmed in a follow-up
telephone call with his father, Dr. Charles Kavenaugh.

43. "The Metropolitan Opens With A Russian Opera," LIFE,
December 6, 1943, pp .36-37.

44. The original negative is numbered 1 of 6,500 originals in
the Weegee Archive and Collection at ICP.

quantity of diamonds in evidence at a wartime opening of the Met, but the bejeweled ladies are aware only of Weegee's clicking camera."[41] For his part, Weegee told
the story that he "discovered" the woman viewing the opera patrons after the negative had been developed, never revealing the prank, saying it was as much a sur-
prise to him as to anyone.

Ironically, this photograph was used by the Nazis in World War II as propaganda.
During the invasion of Anzio, Italy, in late 1943, Charles Kavenaugh was sitting in a
foxhole when out of the skies came leaflets reproducing "The Critic." Inscribed
underneath the image were the words, "GIs, is this what you're fighting for?" Kavenaugh remembers being too embarrassed to mention to anyone that the woman in
the photograph was his grandmother.[42]

The photograph was first published in LIFE magazine, with the caption "The fashionable people were laden with jewels. Most bejeweled were Mrs. George W. Kavenaugh and Lady Decies whose entry was viewed with distaste by spectator."[43] The
photograph that LIFE printed, which is the version most often reproduced, is only
one third of the original negative.[44] On the opposite page from the women arriving

"The Critic," November 22, 1943, first
published in LIFE, December 6, 1943

Installation view of Weegee's exhibition in "Art in
Progress," Museum of Modern Art, New York, 1944

at the opera was another photograph by Weegee taken during the performance of
the opera with the caption, "The plain people waited in line for hours to get standing room, listened intently and, as always, showed better musical manners than
people sitting in boxes." This contrast of images, the rich with the jewels, and the
well-mannered "plain people," was exactly what Weegee was striving for in all of
his photography. The incongruence of life, between the rich and poor, the victims
and the rescued, the murdered and the living — his photographs had the ability to
make us all eyewitnesses and voyeurs. The first time the photo appeared with the
actual title, "The Critic," was in Weegee's own book, *Naked City*.[45]

### Naked City

*"History… is, indeed, little more than the register of crimes, follies, and misfortunes of
mankind."*[46]

Weegee had achieved some critical attention for several photographs which
appeared in two exhibitions at the Museum of Modern Art in 1943 and 1944, enti-

45. Naked City, pp. 130-131.

46. Edward Gibbon (1737-1794), The Decline and Fall of
the Roman Empire, 1776, vol. 1, ch. 3, p. 69, reprinted by
Random House, New York, 1958.

tled "Action Photography" and "Art in Progress," respectively.[47] Unlike the exhibitions he had at the Photo League, these were the first occasions when Weegee's photographs were being seen in the context of an art museum. His photograph "The Critic" became the center of attention of the "Art in Progress" exhibition. When Weegee heard about the commotion, he returned to the museum to make a story in photographs of viewer reactions to his masterwork. *PM* finally published "The Critic" with five other photographs by Weegee of viewers of this image in the *PM Picture Magazine*, as "A Weegee Gets Attention at Museum of Modern Art."[48] During this time the *Saturday Evening Post* columnist Earl Wilson gave Weegee the moniker "O. Henry with a camera."[49]

In the months following the first MoMA exhibition, a number of his colleagues at *PM* and several personal friends suggested that he consider creating a digest of his best photographs for publication. What was obvious to others had really not occurred to him, but Weegee would try almost anything to get his name and photographs additional public attention. In late 1943, Weegee began to show the digest to publishers for potential sponsorship. He was rejected with the standard reply, "Who would buy a book of seedy photographs of New York?"[50] William McCleery, the editor of *PM*, listened to Weegee's complaints about how his book idea was being rejected, and suggested that *PM* should undertake the enterprise of publishing it. McCleery offered to make a call to a friend at Essential Books, which led to its publication. By June of 1945, *Naked City* began to appear in the stores.

*Naked City* was an immediate and overwhelming success. Although it was small in format, $9\frac{1}{4} \times 6\frac{1}{2}$ inches, it was replete with eighteen chapters reproducing 229 gravure images, and sold for four dollars. The paper was slightly coated so the ink trapped well, thus giving the blacks a deep, rich, velvety quality. Within the first six months of publication, *Naked City* went through six printings.

In his foreword to the book, McCleery makes several important statements to reinforce Weegee's intentions. "He will take his camera and ride off in search of new evidence that his city, even in her most drunken and disorderly and pathetic moments, is beautiful." Later in the introduction he reiterates this theme. "He remains as shy and sensitive as if he had spent his life photographing babies and bridesmaids. This, I think, is further evidence that he has been inspired not by a taste for sensationalism but by his love for the city and her children — especially the troubled and unfortunate ones, the kitten-loving ones who sleep on fire escapes in the summer."[51]

*Naked City* was reviewed in all the New York dailies and most of the weekly news and cultural magazines, and covered the entire windows of Brentano's and Scribner's bookstores. The reviews of *Naked City* were extremely favorable, calling Weegee a "poet with a camera," "The Little Man Who's Always There," and proclaiming, "Weegee today is Art, as his new book, *Naked City* attests it."[52] Without exception, every reviewer wrote more about Weegee than his photographs; he was now perceived as grand a character as any of the people he photographed. However, the *New York Times*, which rarely purchased photographs from Weegee, was not as kind. Russell Maloney's review, which appeared on July 22, 1945, began by saying, "The New York news photographer whose annoying whim it is to call himself Weegee offers in *Naked City*, 200-odd excellent pictures of Manhattan scenes, along with some rather uninspiring captions and text." He goes on to say, "Weegee has managed to accumulate a number of pictures of recently dead, but none the less

47. "*Action Photography,*" August 17 through September 19, 1943, and "Art in Progress," May 24 through September 17, 1944.

48. PM Daily, *Friday, June 2, 1944, p. 16.*

49. "*Weegee*" by Earl Wilson, Saturday Evening Post, *May 22, 1943, p. 37.*

50. *From an unpublished manuscript version of* Weegee by Weegee, *in the Weegee Archive at ICP.*

51. Naked City, *pp. 6-7.*

52. *Reviews from* Time, *July 23, 1945, p. 71,* Saturday Review of Literature, *July 28, 1945, p. 17, and* Newsweek, *July 23, 1945, p.74.*

very dead, people. He seems very proud of these, but they are not the best thing in the book."

Weegee began a series of book signings and radio interviews, and many of the photographs were syndicated around the world; he eventually went on a national lecture tour. When he would arrive in each city along the tour, the newspaper hosting his visit would run a contest. Most often, the prize would be an evening with Weegee, riding around the respective city in a police car, with Weegee and the police driver acting as hosts and tour guides. Weegee was riding on a wave of fame that he had always dreamed of, and he was enjoying it. Wherever he went during the second half of 1945, giving lectures, radio interviews, or personal appearances, he was hailed as a *cause célèbre*.

A review of *Naked City* in *Newsweek* attributed to Weegee a statement that foretold the second half of his career. "Weegee the Famous is currently working on another book about New York City, but 'Different from anything anybody's done before. My own interpretation of the city, no cops, no murders, no fires.'"[53] Less than a year later, in an interview that took place from his hospital bed in Bellevue Hospital after minor surgery, he reiterated this theme. "I'm never going to make news photos any more. I'm not going to take fires, or fights or accidents. That isn't the New York that I love now. That's the seamy side. I've cut that out."[54]

A year later, Weegee's second book had been published, *Weegee's People*.[55] Although it was not nearly as successful as *Naked City*, it was the book he said he wanted to make — no murders, no fires, no grim reminders of urban disorder, for the most part, just ordinary people engaged in the lighter side of life in New York. His publisher arranged several book signings and lecture tours on the East Coast. While in Boston signing books in late 1946, Weegee met Margaret Atwood, a quiet woman from a family who had real estate interests. In February of the next year, Weegee and Margaret were married in New York, and they moved to Hollywood the following November.[56]

### Weegee the Filmmaker and Actor

Sometime in the early 1940s, through his friend Francis Lee, an independent filmmaker associated with the Photo League, Weegee was introduced to the 16mm handheld camera. Weegee was interested in expanding his repertoire in photography, but it was not until after the publication of *Naked City* that he became seriously involved with making motion pictures. The showing of his first film took place at the New School for Social Research in 1946, entitled *Manhattan Moods*. Lasting sixteen minutes, it featured his mechanically altered and distorted views of Coney Island, and various night shots of Manhattan.[57]

In 1946, a year after the publication of *Naked City*, the Hollywood film producer Mark Hellinger sent word to Essential Books that he was interested in purchasing the rights to the title of Weegee's first book. After several months of negotiations, handled by Weegee's older brother, Elias, who was a lawyer, a contract was signed which included a payment of approximately $3,000, a position for Weegee as a consultant to the film, and a small part as a news photographer. Production began in the spring of 1947, and *The Naked City* was to have the distinction of being one of the first feature films shot largely on the streets of New York. Weegee was completely enthralled by the large-scale, Hollywood-style production of *Naked City*. Having given up news photography just one year earlier, he decided Hollywood

53. *Reviewer unidentified,* Newsweek, *July 23, 1945, p. 76.*

54. *"Why Weegee won't marry a Brooklyn girl,"* PM Picture Magazine, *April 21, 1946, p. 5.*

55. Weegee's People, *New York: Duell, Sloan, & Pearce/Essential Books, 1946.*

56. *"Weegee's Wedding," by Marc J. Parsons,* Minicam Photography, *June 1947. On page 100 of* Weegee by Weegee, *he contradicts the truth by saying, "Since I had no wife of my own, a sound man at the RKO studios presented me with his."*

57. *In 1948 the film was expanded to 20 minutes and was renamed* Weegee's New York.

"Weegee, as Clown, Covers Circus From the Inside," July 9, 1943

58. The Naked City, Universal Pictures, 1948, black and white, 96 minutes, directed by Jules Dassin, starring Barry Fitzgerald and Howard Duff.

would be his next address, and the film business his next profession. [58]

Arriving in Hollywood, Weegee had lofty hopes of making it big in the film industry. He joined the Screen Actors Guild in early 1948, and over the next four years received bit parts, usually playing some kind of lower-class denizen of New York — a press or street photographer (*The Naked City*, 1948, and *Every Girl Should Be Married*, 1948), a timekeeper at a boxing match (*The Set Up*, 1949), a taxi cab driver (*The Yellow Cab Man*, 1950), and a bum in a Skid Row mission (*Journey into Light*, 1951), familiar territory for Weegee since these characters were very much like the people he had photographed. Weegee was separated from Margaret in 1949, with his acting career going nowhere in a hurry.

### The Distortions
Knowing something about camera lenses and special effects from his first film, Weegee began advertising himself as a technical consultant. He found some success in this area of the film business, but it was not enough to sustain him. With time on his hands because little acting or consulting work could be found, Weegee began to

produce a series of distorted photographs, based on the lens he had devised for his 1948 film *Weegee's New York,* and from his experiments begun in the Acme darkrooms.[59]

There were three basic methods Weegee used to create these distortions. Weegee's first experiments were made by placing a textured or curved glass or other translucent material (Blumenfeld says he began with the bottoms of broken milk bottles) between the enlarger lens and the photographic paper. This effect would alter the image of the negative to varying degrees depending on the density, pattern, or texture of the material he used. He also tried manipulating or mutilating copy negatives by placing them in boiling water, or melting them with an open flame. The third method he employed involved making multiple exposures from the same or various negatives, moving the same piece of photographic paper after each exposure. Given his darkroom talent, he sometimes combined these techniques. Weegee later added a system by which he would affix a kaleidoscope to the end of the camera lens, or use it to replace the camera lens, letting the refractive designs multiply what the camera would have ordinarily recorded as a single image. From this period until his death, Weegee concentrated on what he alternately called his "distortions," "caricatures," "creative photography," or most often, his "art."

While in Hollywood, Weegee had compiled a series of images of the film community which eventually became his third book, *Naked Hollywood.*[60] It is Weegee at his most depthless humor, with the photographs being equally undistinguished. By comparison with his first two publications, *Naked Hollywood* was a farce and financial failure. Filled with disdain, *Naked Hollywood* was his caustic anticlimactic statement about his excursion to the West Coast. However, the book did become one of the first outlets for his distortions, mixing them with straight photographs — usually portraits of Hollywood celebrities or immediately recognizable images of Los Angeles.

Weegee returned to New York in 1952 and rented a room over a Chinese restaurant on Ninth Avenue and 47th Street. He continued to work on his distortion series, only taking editorial assignments when he wasn't out pushing his "creative" photography, or when there was a financial necessity. The photo editors at the newspapers and magazines who had published his portraits of New York in the previous two decades were most often apathetic to his distortions. They considered them curiosities, not the hard-edge photographs Weegee had become known for; many of the editors would publish them just to appease him.

It was also during this period that Weegee was producing a series of photographs and stories that bordered on pornography. Working out of a studio on West 57th Street, he attended and also taught classes on how to photograph the nude female figure. On other occasions he would lead field trips to Fire Island with paid models to further this cause.[61] The results of these sessions were often reproduced in a number of popular men's magazines of the time, *Stag, True Detective, Art Photography: Sophistication in Pictures,* and the short-lived *Photographers Showplace,* where Weegee also served as the photo editor.

Even before he left New York for the West Coast, Weegee was a regular at most of the midtown Manhattan camera stores, making the rounds, trying to get samples of anything the stores were trying to promote. Now back in New York, Weegee actively worked on promoting himself and his camera techniques. He was not above showing up at almost every camera manufacturer's demonstration, and occa-

59. "Weegee: Alias Arthur Fellig," p. 23.

60. Naked Hollywood, *New York: Pellegrini & Cudahy,* 1953, edited by Mel Harris.

61. *Author's interviews with Kingdon Lane, November 27, 1995, and John Morrin, December 18, 1995.*

sionally was hired to show slides of his past work. In general, Weegee took every opportunity to unveil his latest darkroom creation, bringing copies of his books for sale and autographing. Weegee would scrounge from the stores or the camera companies their newest product, be it lens, film, paper, or chemistry. Whether it was something he could use or not, he loved to say to an audience, "I endorse this product," then move the microphone away from his mouth, continuing, "But I don't recommend it."[62]

During the 1950s and 1960s, Weegee earned income by reissuing the photographs which made him famous from the 1930s and 1940s. Often, the photographs were used in publications as varied as automobile insurance company newsletters and brochures illustrating first-aid procedures for the Red Cross.[63] He would often have others print from his negatives, either because he was tired of darkroom work, or because requests for his prints were purely an economic undertaking. Although he makes reference to his "allergy" to telephones, he had a huge network of individuals he called on. Among the papers Weegee saved are forty-three pocket- and desk-size personal telephone directories.[64]

Weegee continued to be generous, always available and able to give a few dollars to a friend in need, and answering technical questions about his photographs or photography in general whenever he lectured or gave demonstrations. It was also during the 1950s and 1960s that Weegee wrote a number of technical manuals and publications on how to make "creative photographs."[65]

### The Final Years
Weegee never enjoyed an extended period of financial security, and in 1957, to make matters worse, he was diagnosed with diabetes. His weakened condition necessitated a move from his apartment into a large room on the first floor of a brownstone on 47th Street, owned by his longtime friend Wilma Wilcox. Weegee had met Wilma at the Photo League in the early 1940s, when she was studying photography to better document her activities while working towards a degree in Psychiatric Social Work at the New York School of Social Work. Wilma later became the Executive Director of the Metropolitan Center for Mental Health in New York. Weegee also knew her socially through mutual friends, often attending parties at Wilma's apartment in Greenwich Village during the 1940s, and again after his return from Hollywood.

Although Weegee and Wilma were never married, they shared a mutual admiration, respect, and relationship which lasted until Weegee's death on December 25, 1968. It was Wilma who was most responsible for continuing the legacy of Weegee. She was a constant supporter of his photography, and if not for Wilma, many of Weegee's prints, negatives, and other personal effects would have been lost during the last years of his life.

Up until the end of his life, Weegee's thoughts on photography remained constant. Photography was something of a game, a racket, a tool that one could exploit. In Weegee's case he used it to document what was around him, always believing that his photographs would have broad appeal, and treating his subject matter fairly. Weegee made the average New Yorker a star in his images, on a par with the society dames and the "swells." He held a mirror up to New York and revealed a city that was provocative and gripping, while at the same time managing to capture the City's heart.

62. Author's interview with George Gilbert, November 4, 1996.

63. Author's interview with Julian Belin, May 14, 1996.

64. Weegee by Weegee, pp. 64-65.

65. Weegee's Secrets of Shooting with Photo Flash, New York: Designers 3, Artist's Publishers, Hartis Publishers, 1953; Weegee's Creative Camera, Garden City: Hanover House, 1959; and Weegee's Creative Photography, London: Ward, Lock, and Co., Ltd., 1964.

Weegee could easily be described as one of the most important freelance photojournalists who ever worked in the profession. Although the last years of his life were melancholy, what he accomplished, in one decade of news photography, from the mid-1930s through the mid-1940s, is an extraordinary chronicle of New York. The publication of his epic, *Naked City,* will always be considered a classic love affair between a photographer and his subject. In Weegee's case, the subject was New York, and his photographs became the frozen moments that are the icons of urban life in its calm, joy, and chaos during that period.

"Max is rushing in the morning's bagels to a restaurant on Second Avenue for the morning trade," c. 1940

"Cafeteria on East Broadway," September 12, 1941

38    "Invitation to the dance," Rehearsal, Yiddish Theater, September 30, 1945

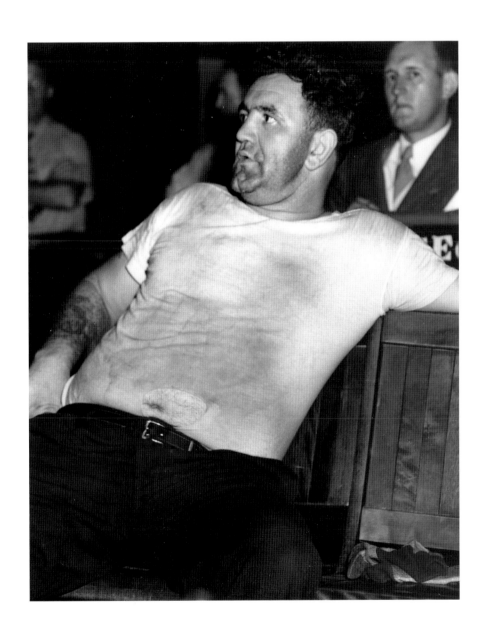

*The janitor takes time out to watch the rehearsal*
*at the Yiddish Theater.* September 30, 1945

*Caffé Bella Napoli*, Little Italy, July, 1944

*A taste of home*, Greek Restaurant, July, 1943

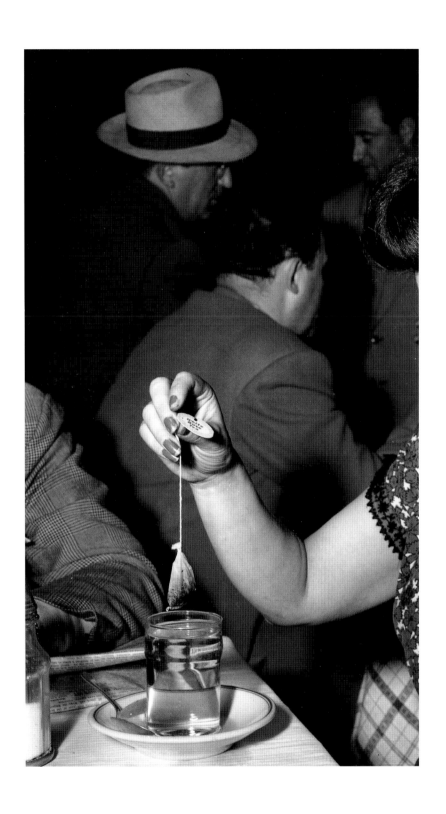

*Tea break at the Café Royal on Second Avenue, meeting place for Yiddish Theater actors,*
September 30, 1945

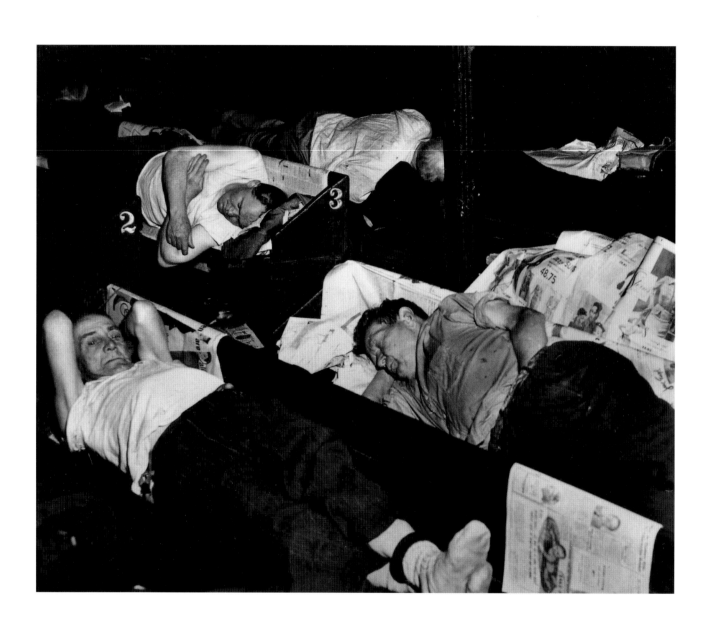

*Doyer Street Mission*, January 21, 1941

*U. S. Hotel at 263 Bowery, c. 1944*

"The Bowery, in all night mission, men sit on benches, … some thinking," December 26, 1940

*A man without legs and his cat, c. 1939*

*Drunken men in the Bowery, c. 1943*

46    *Heat spell*, May 23, 1941

*Tenement sleeping, June, 1943*          *Sleeping on the Fire Escape, c. 1939*          47

*Summer, the Lower East Side, c. 1937*

*Welcome Home, Jimmy, July 12, 1943*

*V-J Day Rally in Little Italy,* September 2, 1945

*The Juggler*, Lower East Side, July, 1940

*Gunman Killed by Off Duty Cop at 344 Broome St.,* February 3, 1942

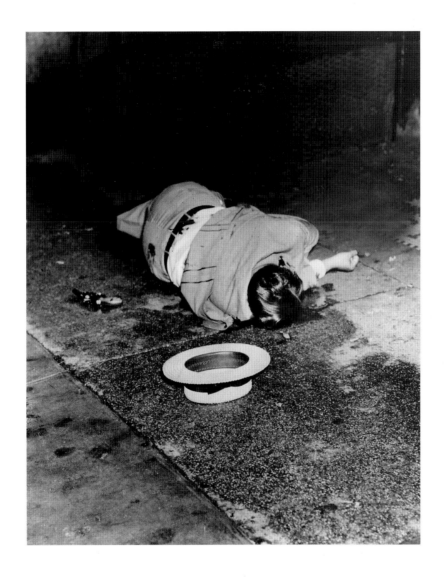

"Murder on the Roof," August 14, 1941        "Corpse with Revolver," August 7, 1936      55

"On the Spot," c. 1940

"Slum Clearance Project. Hell's Kitchen"

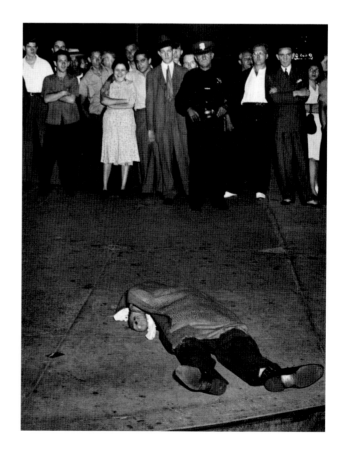

"Rocco Finds His Pal Stabbed," July 31, 1941
"Who Done That?"

*Auto accident victim,* 1938

"This was a friendly game of Bocci," c. 1939

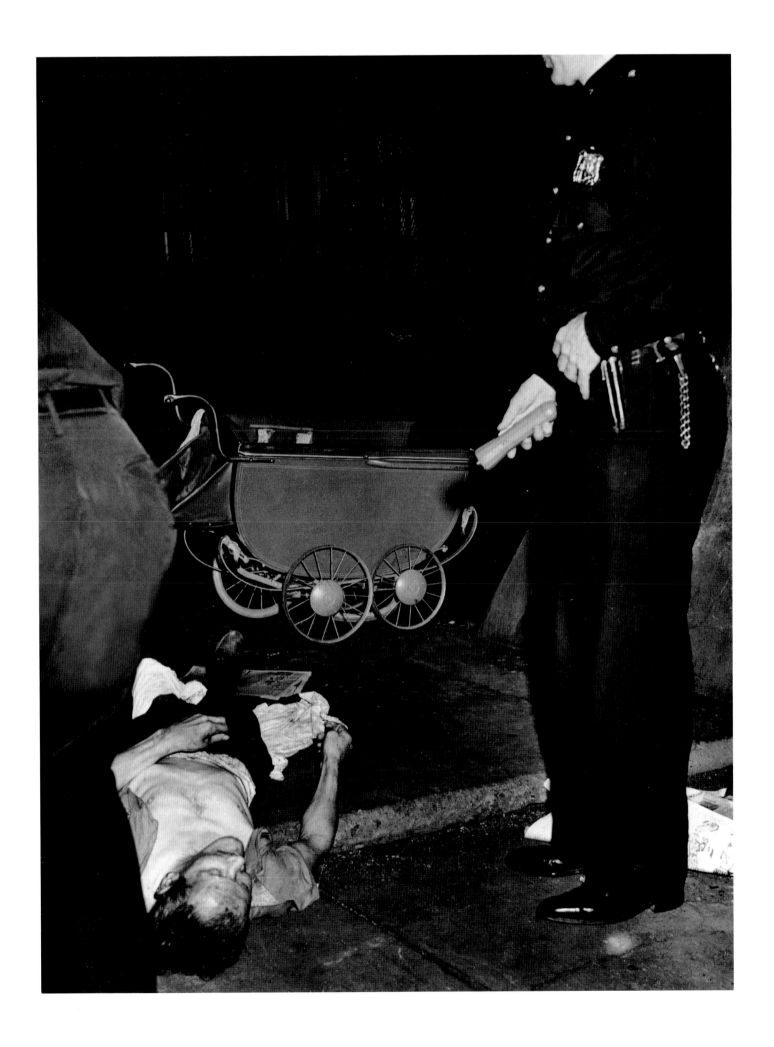

"One-way Ride," 1940

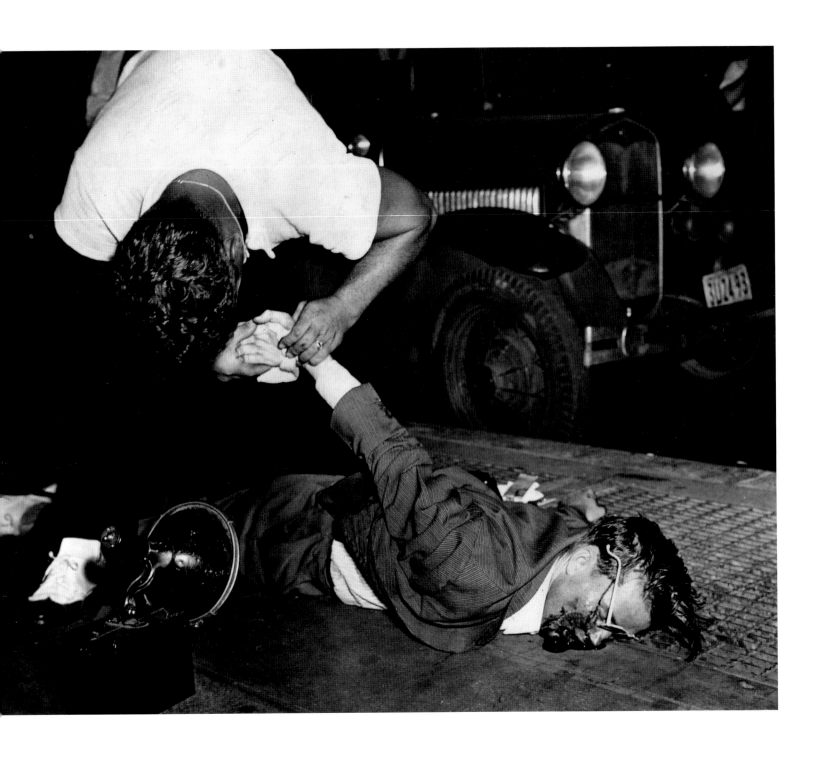

*Bandit*, August 11, 1941

"Joy of Living," April 17, 1942

"Murder in Hell's Kitchen," c. 1940

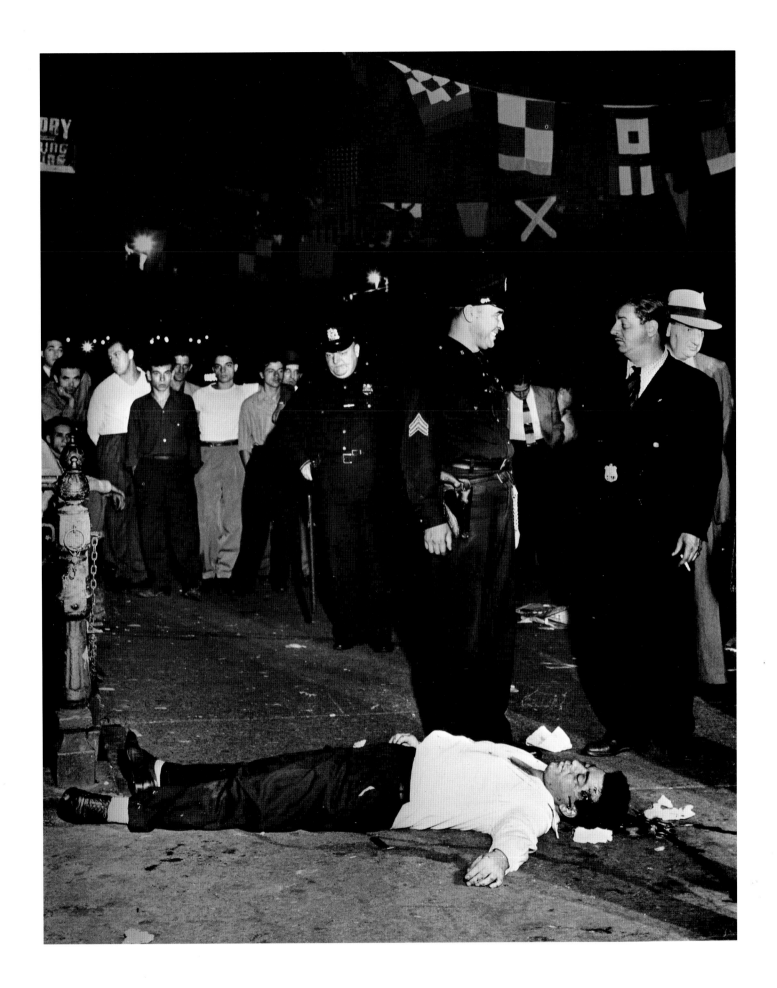

*Murder at the Feast of San Gennaro, September 22, 1939*

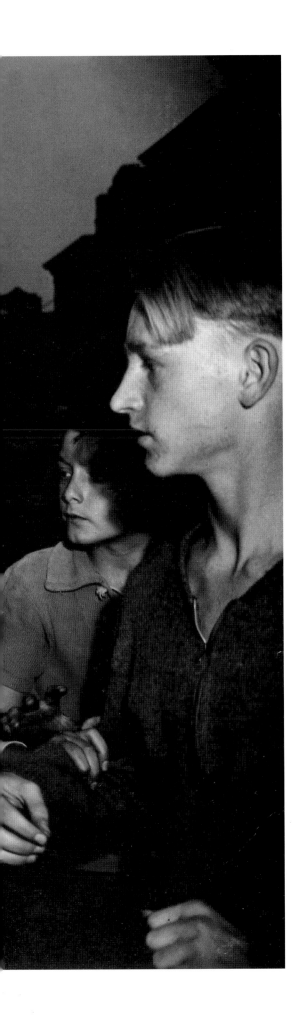

"Their First Murder," October 9, 1941

"Here he is as he was left in the gutter...
He's got a DOA tied his arm, that means 'Dead On Arrival'," c. 1941

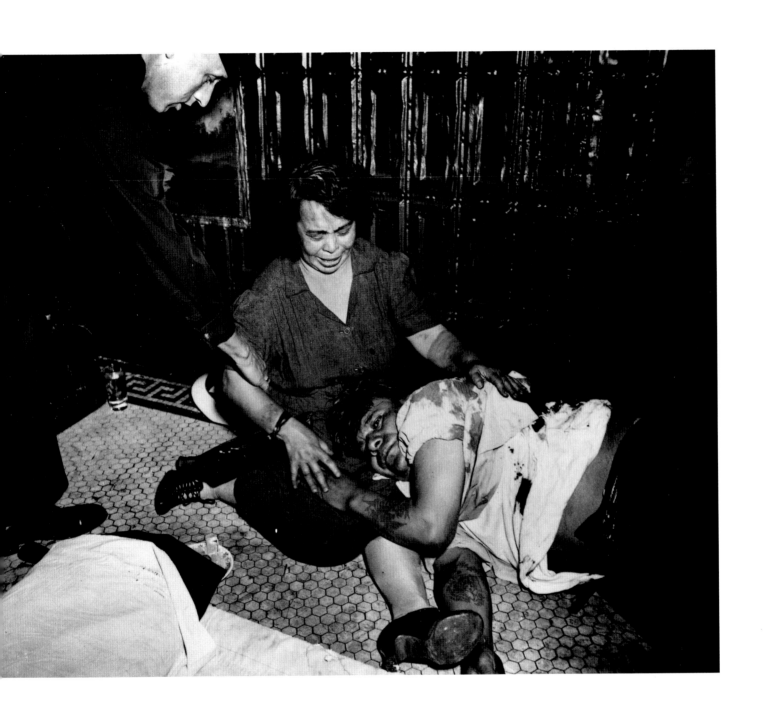

*Manuelda Hernandez holds Manuel Jiminez in Her Lap, July 30, 1941*

*Victim of Auto Accident Waiting for Doctor, September 25, 1940*

Photographer unknown. *Weegee with poster for the film,* The Naked City, 1949

**Weegee and Film Noir** Alain Bergala

Weegee's first book, *Naked City*, was published in 1945, the year in which the best films noirs of the forties — *Gilda*, *The Big Sleep*, *The Blue Dahlia*, *Fallen Angel*, *The Killers*, *The Postman Always Rings Twice* — were for the most part in either pre-production or production. The phrase *film noir* was not coined until the next year, by French journalists who had discovered, en masse, the American films they had been unable to see during the German occupation. The category was named after the fact: most film historians agree on 1941, the year of John Huston's *Maltese Falcon*, as the year of birth of this new genre, which followed immediately upon that of the "gangster movies" that flourished in the thirties.

### *The Naked City* — The Film

Mark Hellinger had produced Robert Siodmak's 1946 film noir, *The Killers*; in 1947, Hellinger hired the screenwriter Martin Wald to write an unusual detective story. He wanted his city, New York, to be the subject, as central as the customary tracking down of the criminal. He meant to inscribe his fiction into a quasi-documentary New York reality, shooting on location whenever possible. Wald submitted a treatment for a police procedural that he titled *Homicide*, and brought Hellinger Weegee's book, which had just come out. Hellinger was first intrigued by the book's title, *Naked City*, which he decided to use for the film. Instead of buying the rights to the title, he more cannily hired Weegee as still photographer. Jules Dassin, the director, maintained that the film was ruined in the editing. During this period, one of the cowriters, Albert Maltz, was jailed by the "executioners" of the witch hunt that had just begun raging in Hollywood, and *The Naked City*, which the censors viewed as particularly suspect, was tarred with the same brush. Despite its genuine originality — which lies essentially in a few scenes shot in the streets of New York, with the camera hidden in a van or behind two-way mirrors — *The Naked City* is not an undisputed masterpiece of film noir. Nevertheless, it owes Weegee more than its title: there are street shots in it that are directly inspired by photographs of his, in particular a lovely "neorealist" scene, recalling well-known photographs by Weegee on the same subject, in which children joyously take advantage of the boon of water spraying from a fire hydrant, until a city bureaucrat comes to close down the fun. Usually there is no place for children in the futureless film noir universe. In *The Naked City*, however, probably due to the influence of Weegee's photographs, the streets of New York are teeming with children jumping rope and roller-skating, barely noticing the pursuit of criminals through the territory of their games. Despite these somewhat forced efforts to inscribe the (weak) police investigation into the real city setting, the documentary shots too often remain unrelated to the fiction. Even the police-car chase across the city, in final pursuit of the killer, uses the old-fashioned rear-projection process. In terms of the inscription of fiction into an immediate reality, Jules Dassin remained light-years behind the revolution that Roberto Rossellini had wrought two years earlier in Italy with *Open City* (*Roma, città aperta*; 1945).

### A Unique Coincidence

There was thus nothing glorious about the meeting of Weegee and cinema, born of the producer's machinations more than from any real artistic recognition, although it must have represented, to this "self-made immigrant's son" straight out of the American myth, the flattering vision that had seduced so many detective-story writers (badly in need of money and legitimacy) or just writers, period, even if most of them were soon disenchanted by the industrial constraints of the great global moviemaking machine.

Weegee spent several years in Hollywood, as a consultant and an actor (in particular, his silhouette is recognizable in Robert Wise's *Set-Up,* of 1949). But what is interesting about the intersection of Weegee's work and American film noir is not the (minor) objective part the photographer played in Hollywood between 1948 and 1952. Rather, it lies in one of those historic, rare coincidences, rich with implications for the parallel history of the arts, by which two only apparently related expressions — in this case, photography and cinema; in the fifties, jazz and cinema; in the sixties, literature and cinema — for a time happen to be at the same outposts of the representation of a period and of a change of ways of thinking that seek further new forms and rhythms to manifest them.

**A Portrait of Weegee as Private Eye**

The gangster films of the thirties tended to be told in the third person. The budding film noir diverged from this objective narrative mode, borrowing from the detective novel the "I" of the private detective who improvises his way through the troubled waters of the big city at night, from one chapter to the next, one encounter to the next, one setting to the next, with neither the foreshadowing nor the overview of an omniscient and omnipresent narrator. The forties were the years of the private detective, whether his name was Sam Spade, if he came from a Dashiell Hammett novel (*The Maltese Falcon*, by John Huston); Philip Marlowe, if from one of Raymond Chandler's (*Murder, My Sweet*, by Edward Dmytryk, 1944; *The Blue Dahlia*, by George Marshall, 1946; *The Big Sleep*, by Howard Hawks, 1946; *Lady in the Lake*, by Robert Montgomery, 1946); or Mike Hammer, if from one of Mickey Spillane's (*Kiss Me Deadly*, by Robert Aldrich, 1955).

Physically, Weegee was built more like those stocky actors with working-class bodies who played the bad boys of the thirties gangster movies — like James Cagney and George Raft — than like the type of actor that the forties film noir would present as the masculine ideal: the subtle, impassive, aristocratic detective à la Humphrey Bogart. And yet, if we were to imagine that we know no more about Weegee's physical appearance than about that of E. J. Bellocq, the faceless photographer of the Storyville prostitutes, how would we picture the man who looked at the night city if we knew him only from his photographs?

Philip Marlowe would be a good guess, from his way of moving through the city, of looking at its shabbiness and squalor, even though Raymond Chandler's detective is a Los Angeleno. No surprises: at the very end of the thirties, while Weegee's flash was crackling in the New York night, Chandler was writing *The Big Sleep* and *Farewell, My Lovely*. Both were giving birth to truly innovative works, outside the beaten tracks of the higher forms of their mediums, at first to earn a living, and far from any cultural legitimacy: Weegee never allowed himself to be intimidated by the code of the "beautiful photograph," which in his day defined the territory of the "art" photo; Chandler began to write at forty-five because he was fired from his job, and published his first texts in the subliterary world of the pulp magazines, for a penny a word, convinced that "it's a trade that you learn like any other."

"Police End Kids' Street Shower — Under
Orders," August 18, 1944

Weegee was not an official police photographer, one of those who records and
delivers evidence (instruments of the crime, suspects and bodies, clues), their flashes puncturing the night in so many film noir sequences in which the police go to
the scene of the crime after the body is discovered. Nor was he a photographer
who depended upon a single newspaper or press agency. He cut himself a place,
custom-made, amid the guild of his peers. If one analyzes it, that place corresponds
fairly closely to that of the private eye in the whodunits of the thirties and the
films noirs of the forties: independent and slightly *beside the law*. Weegee was proud
of being the only photographer to have obtained the privilege of installing a police
radio in his famous Chevrolet. Neither outlaw nor representative of the law: just
*close enough to the law*, like the private eye, to benefit from the encroachment on
liberties (to be where ordinary citizens are prohibited from going) and the speed
of intervention granted its agents, yet *detached enough from the law* to remain
fiercely free and independent, not aggregated.

Like the private eye's, his journey to the end of the night took him through settings both varied and monotonous in their repetition: the gleaming streets, the sea-

green backyards, the small bars of the down-and-out, but also the nightclubs with their untidy dressing rooms, where the girls came to change hurriedly between two numbers. But we could say that the photographer goes from shot to shot, with no apparent concern for telling a story, resolving a puzzle. It is precisely one of the characteristics of film noir that it dared, with a fine carelessness, to neglect cinema's earlier requirements of logical sequences of scenes and information. The viewer is very often launched into the logic of a dream or nightmare, in which causal relations relax into more mysterious sequences, reveries of a more delirious or nocturnal kind. Upon leaving the projection, the viewer forgets the screenplay's hazy final explanations, remembering only, indelibly, a few unforgettable images, a few disconnected scenes, a few visual flashes that are, in the end, as erratic as photographs in a book of prose.

There is a famous anecdote that tells how Howard Hawks, unable to answer a question of Bogart's, and himself lost in the byways of *The Big Sleep*'s intrigue, telephoned the novel's author, after the co-screenwriter William Faulkner gave up. Chandler sent a cable in which he serenely admitted that he didn't know who killed the character in question either. "By nature," he wrote in a letter of 1957, "I am a discursive writer, who falls in love with a scene, a character, a setting, or an atmosphere." As for Howard Hawks, he would say of *The Big Sleep*: "It was the first time that I made a film stating once and for all that I would not explain anything. I was just trying to make good scenes."

In this acceptance of narrative disconnection, forties film noir approached the logic of a collection of photographs like *Naked City*: the very significant general atmosphere matters more than the story, the fragments matter more than their narrative connection. But though this is true of film noir conceived as a cluster rather than a collection of individual films, it does not explain why this noir cluster (as such, undifferentiated) does not enter so intensely into phase before Weegee's particular photographic oeuvre.

### Weegee Makes His Own Movies

The explanation is that he was the only photographer of his age to cover the *other side of the path*, where his photography approached cinema, the cinema that was strictly his contemporary: film noir. It is not only that his subjects — simply because they reflect the same side of the reality of an age — are often the same as those of *cinéma noir*, but that his way of photographing is singularly cinematic, generating fictional effects, *on the borderline* between the two territories.

You have only to look at one or another photo in which Weegee shot *from behind* the subject who was presumably making the mob of press photographers run: a nightclub dancer obligingly posing; Bette Davis or some other star at some wonderful opening. Weegee was not gregarious; if there was any competition, he was instinctively reluctant to return to the area assigned to the photographers, facing the subject, from the "correct angle," which he willingly ceded to his colleagues. So much for the "salable" magazine photo of Bette Davis (the one all the other photographers present were taking): his would show, from the back, only the star's hair and fur coat. Like a good filmmaker, he was really interested in neither the actress nor the photographs, but rather the interval between the two poles, and the history (of dulled desire, good-natured nonsense, and gregarious clinkers) that this interval, and only this interval, tells. In the history of the visual arts, it was cinema that made the back a privileged part of the representation of the body, because of the many shots in which two actors are facing each other, and the concomitant traveling shots beforehand. Weegee is a great *photographieur* of backs.

His taste for reverse shots — an eminently cinematic concept — often made him shoot his subject in a reverse angle, so that he tended to diverge from the field of the "photographable" in any given situation. At a concert he was as inspired by the reverse shot of the audience as by the shot of singers with their mouths open, disfigured by their effort (the beautiful is produced by the ugly). Ignoring the grand spectacle of a building in flames, he deliberately photographed the reverse shot of those watching.

Just like filmmakers, Weegee was fascinated by Black Marias, like small, Italian-style theaters, their scrap-metal curtains perforated like the partition of a confessional. He often photographed — from the sidewalk, from the standpoint of the viewer in the street — the absurd kings and queens of the night who were in them, dethroned in some police roundup, yet displaying themselves to his camera's gaze like actors appearing for a last curtain call on this improvised stage, before ending the night at their station. He could not resist the temptation to change the angle, to go wedge himself with his camera at the back of the van, so as to get the opposite point of view on the scene, of those loaded on by the police: of the subjective camera of misfortune, when the door of the morgue drawer closes on the viewer and on the young dead woman of *Kiss Me Deadly*. At night, on a beach frequented by lovers, he aimed his camera, loaded with infrared film, at the entwined couples, then changed the angle by 180 degrees, training it on a young woman in exactly his own position, that of the voyeur, just as Alfred Hitchcock, at the end of *Rear Window* (1954), turned the camera, which this time was moving along with the murderer, toward the voyeur, contrary to all the previous shots.

When you look at a lot of Weegee's photographs, you more often feel that you're looking at frames of a movie, caught on film as the camera moves, than at photographs individually centered, as images in themselves. The scale of his shots and his concept of framing are more cinematic than photographic. And therein, undoubtedly, lies the source of the fictional effect of many of his photos. Where another photographer would have chosen the distance and framing to allow the clearest reading of the subject (for example, a body on the sidewalk), Weegee often gives the impression of having framed too widely or too tightly, or else from a slightly clumsy angle, *as if the equilibrium of the picture was waiting for something offscreen to enter the shot* (for example, the feet that will come to fill the too-empty space around the body mentioned above). Quite often, there is in the very imbalance of his shots a reference to offscreen that gives his photographs their quality of lack, which provides an anchorage for the onlooker's fictional imagination.

Weegee also sometimes practices the metonymic framing of cinema's tight shots: of a violent event — a murder or an accident — we only see the chalk outline that describes the absence of a body, or the absurdity of a single shoe jammed under the tire of a perfectly motionless car. He was not afraid to shoot, director-style, just the legs of two characters, whose faces we are left to imagine, forever offscreen, as in the terrifying sequence in *Kiss Me Deadly* in which Robert Aldrich filmed a scene of torture and the murder of the young hitchhiker, showing us only the legs of tormentors and victim.

Even when he chose a long shot, Weegee's shot was more like moviemaking than like press photography. By framing slightly too widely, he often deprived us of a part of the legibility of the subject's central scene — a poor, anonymous hero of

*Accident victim under 3rd Ave. Elevated train, 1939*

a fatal news item — that he inscribed instead into a script in which this poor figure, when all is said and done, has no meaning outside his relationship to the urban setting, purified by the light of the flash, which, as in the theater or films noirs, emphasizes only a few edges, a few almost abstract lines. At other times, the slightly too-large frame weaves mysterious, perilous connections between the fallen hero and chance figures (rubberneckers, passersby, police officers, ambulance men) that — like underpaid, awkward extras — have come to complete this picture of the death of an unknown person, to whom, were he the lowest of the low, Weegee nevertheless made the gift of a funeral scene, directed by destiny in a mocking, chancy, piecemeal way, but affirming that, despite everything, this anonymous death deserved the setting of the constellation of signs that is at the basis of any true representation of destiny.

Weegee's "touch" is very largely characterized by his determination to resist the elementary rules of press photos (the correct angle, maximum legibility) in order to frame on the contrary the scenes proposed to him by life's violence, as a director might frame a film shot: in such a way as to leave room for mystery, for speculation. To draw in fiction that will fill in information that is incomplete or imperfect, too partial or too large.

### Compassion, Numen

Raymond Chandler analyzed the altogether odd relationship between the private detective and the stories he passes through, the environments and sufferings that are the daily fare of his work, since it is made up of both implication and exteriority. This is fairly close to the photographer's place in reality: Weegee photographed all the world's grief on the faces of two women who are watching their building burn with their families still inside, then got back into his Chevrolet, heading for another set and other actors of human misery in the big damned city. But the comparison would cease where Chandler says of the private eye: "The detective exists complete, whole, unshaken by anything that might happen; being a detective, he is placed outside and above the story, and it will always be that way." Despite the modesty that led him to project an ostensible coolness that set him apart from the American tradition of the "humanist" photograph, Weegee's photographs all bear the trace of a feeling that is very precisely *compassion*, but free of any display of emotion or sentimentality. The dandyism of the hero of the "hard-boiled" detective novel prohibited his showing any emotion whatsoever in the face of the spectacle of the world's horrors with which his job relentlessly confronts him. The filmmakers tended to share with the characters who acted as their guides in this world full of *terribilitá* an impassivity that prohibited their allowing themselves to be visibly affected even in the filming of such scenes. Any pathos in the representation is deontologically excluded from a true film noir. The film, too, should remain impeccably impassive.

Ostensibly, Weegee the photographer sought to remain as cold as a private eye, allowing not the slightest trace of personal sentimentalism to affect his images. But he constantly betrayed himself by his taste and genius for the "decisive moment," his ability to set off his flash at the exact fraction of a second in which he captured, in grief, in the surrender of all control over posture or gesture, in the moment of the great catastrophes, the "numen" that Roland Barthes so often spoke of, that "emphatic truth of gesture in life's great circumstances," that "excessive pose," that "fixed, eternalized, trapped hysteria, because in the end we keep it immobile, chained with a long gaze…" — that is the mark of Weegee's most famous images.

### Rich and Poor, Flashes of Beauty

Weegee's nighttime runs led him — as surely as did the private detective's investigation into the origin of the evil — to stretch over society's great gap between the down-and-out, the excluded of every kind, and the rich, who attended the openings of movies or opera, great restaurants, and the smart parts of town. Chandler wrote: "Marlowe and I, we do not despise the upper classes because they bathe and have money; we despise them because they ring false." Weegee exposed them because they pose, and, unlike the makers of films noirs (who were often satisfied to reveal their moral "blackness" without attacking their outward image), he could not keep from displaying their ugliness, or from exposing the vulgarity that to his gimlet, piercing eyes was the basic universal truth that lies hidden behind luxury's disguise.

Film, even noir, operates on glamour, seduction (except for a few low-budget or deliberately "dingy" films, such as, at times, Edgar G. Ulmer's *Detour*, 1945, or *Kiss Me Deadly*). The movie private eye is poor, and sometimes sleeps in his office, like Weegee in his car/photo lab, but he is fascinated by the polished gleam with which the erotic seductiveness of luxury especially endows women, and in which he will burn his wings and lose his moral and professional bearings somewhat. Unlike the private eye, Weegee did not see himself as an "out-class" who could as easily be comfortable amid the luxury and refinements of the rich. We have only to see him in the highest company, in photographs taken after his admission to fame, to understand that he was never tempted to mimic belonging to a milieu that he knew was not, nor ever would be, his. Even in the drawing rooms, he remained the Weegee of the street. He seems never to have felt the attraction, or else he protected himself from it, avenging himself on the image of the rich to say as crudely as possible that it is nothing but vulgarity. He literally "deglamourized" everything he photographed — even Marilyn Monroe, who visibly recognized in him a fellow survivor of dire poverty. Undaunted by their prestige, he returned even the powerful of this world to their common vulgarity.

Yet even though Weegee chose to tirelessly photograph horror rather than seductiveness, he was far from insensitive to beauty. He, too, looked for nuggets of beauty as he passed through the night, but elsewhere, where it was not tarted up to allure. For Weegee, beauty could only be captured unawares, in the last place you would expect it, on a fire escape, where the children of the poor sleep huddled, dirty as urchins, rather than in an audience showing off at a Metropolitan Opera premiere, in the detail of a Barthesian *punctum* that miraculously escapes the blackness of the image's spontaneous subject. Beauty, for Weegee, was not a conscious photographic target; it could only be contraband and pinpointed. An unhoped-for flash in the night.

### The Aesthetic, Style, and Émigrés of Central Europe

What is ultimately a very heterogeneous collection of films (the criminal psychology film, the psychoanalytical film, certain exotic films, certain spy films, and so on) is defined as belonging to the single genre of film noir primarily by a visual aesthetic, a style of lighting: strongly contrasted images (at times pure black and white); hard, clearly demarcated shadows; determinedly black areas (totally "stopped down," as they say in filmmaking); strongly directional lighting that reveals its artificial, pinpointing source. Out of a set plunged into blackness, there emerge only a few luminous edges, describing in an inky night an abstract architecture whose details and materials are relegated to a perceptual emptiness. The chief characteristics of "Weegee's touch" are immediately recognizable in these distinguishing features. The aesthetic relationship with Weegee's ruthlessly flashed photographs must be sought on the side of the "poor" lighting of the B-movie films noirs — those with the tightest budgets, such as Ulmer's famous *Detour*, filmed in a week for $30,000 — most of the shots are lit by one or two spotlights; the lighting is direct and raw, with no softening embellishments or diffusion.

There is a very disturbing concordance between the temptation of the overexposure of the brightly lit areas in certain films noirs and the overly lit effects of Weegee's flash on the foregrounds that receive this brutal light with no mediation whatsoever. The image in *Kiss Me Deadly* takes on a maximal gap between bright and low lighting and overexposes the lit areas with a visual violence that may refer back to the famous interrogation scene from Otto Preminger's *Laura* (1944), in which the actress's face is too brightly lit — like the social subjects in some of Weegee's photographs — almost to the point of her features being erased by the director, who hides behind the police brutality to temporarily disfigure Gene Tierney's sweet face. Perhaps the only time that Weegee may have been caught out in a cultural reference was when he compared his flash work to "Rembrandt's style" of lighting from the side.

But this objective meeting between two luminous aesthetics, Weegee's photographs and the B-movie films noirs, arises perhaps from more than just a technical assessment, or from what happened to the American conscience in the decades of the thirties and forties, during which, notes Martin Scorsese, Pandora's box opened and "strange shadows invaded American cinema, a feeling of insecurity, or permanent menace, as if the ground might suddenly fall away under your feet." Weegee was a new American, in that he was born in Galicia and was eleven years old when his family emigrated to the United States, settling on New York City's Lower East Side. Film noir, which constitutes American cinema's most distinctive image, historically arose from the capture of American reality by an aesthetic derived from Expressionism, and made, to a significant extent, by European film people who had foreseen the looming darkness before fleeing Nazism and finding refuge and work in the United States. They were directors (Fritz Lang, Alfred Hitchcock, Otto Preminger, Billy Wilder, Douglas Sirk, Robert Siodmak, Edgar G. Ulmer, André de Toth, John Brahm), technicians (Eugen Schïfftan, Theodor Sparkhul), and actors (Peter Lorre, Fritz Kortner). Although Weegee gave himself over entirely — as man and photographer — to American culture and territory, although he passed himself off as a purely unsocialized and instinctual photographer, resolutely beyond culture, there is a disturbing intersection between the very frequently expressionistic chiaroscuro and filmic settings of his images and the Central European-derived aesthetic that he shares, however reluctantly, with the émigrés of cinema who in large part fashioned the aesthetic of the forties films noirs.

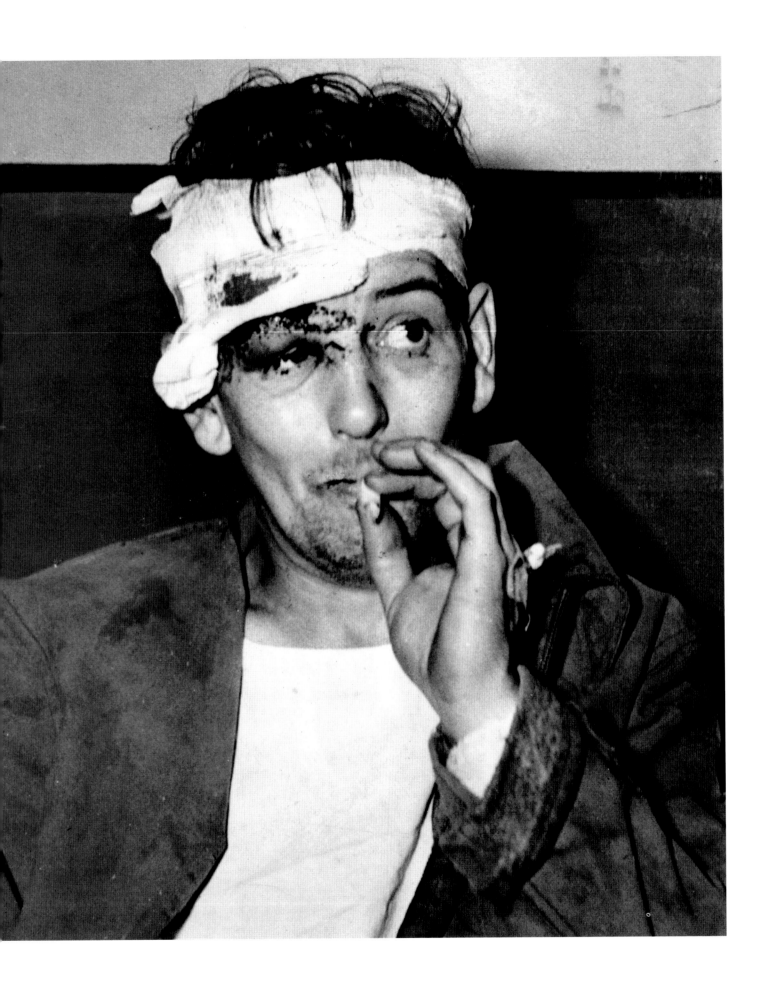

*William Morey, Husband of Woman who Killed Children and Herself, August 28, 1941*

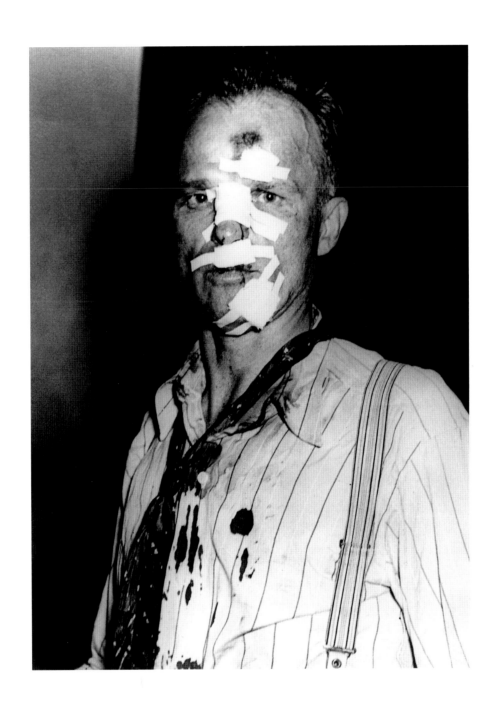

*John Pulko, Accused Attacker Nabbed in Pistol Chase, September 18, 1939*

*Anthony Esposito, Accused "Cop Killer,"*
*January 16, 1941*

*Barber Confesses to Murder of Einer Sporrer, March 21, 1937*

*After Vice Raid*, January 18, 1941

Henry Rosen (left) and Harvey Stemmer (center) were arrested for
bribing basketball players, January 25, 1945

*Frank Pape, Arrested for Homicide, November 10, 1944*

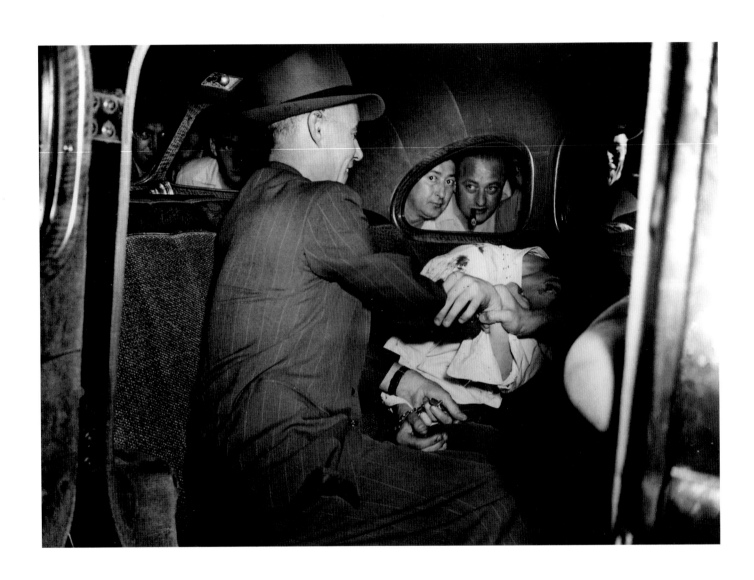

*Harold Horn, Knocked Over Milk Wagon with Stolen Car, June 27, 1941*

*Irma Twiss Epstein, Nurse Accused of Killing a Baby, February 9, 1942*

"These are men arrested for dressing as girls...
the cops, the old meanies broke up their dance... and took them to the pokey," c. 1939

"This boy was arrested for dressing like a girl," c. 1939

"The Gay Deceiver," c. 1939

*Major Green, Arrested for Murder, January 15, 1937*

*Wife of Major Green being escorted out of police station.* January 15, 1937

Unidentified man in handcuffs at police station, c. 1941

"The lineup," 1939

*After the Street Fight*, c. 1940

"A New LOW in Arrests — Midget Seller of French Post Cards Arrested," April 18, 1940

*"Factory Frankie" Aherns (left) and Marty Powell (right) Arrested for Association*, February 17, 1937

*Charles Sodokoff and Arthur Webber Use Their Top Hats to Hide Their Faces*, January 27, 1942

*Man Caught in Store*, February 17, 1941

*Man Caught in Store, Led Away to Radio Car*, February 17, 1941

*Two Passengers Are Killed As Auto Dives Into Hudson,*
January 25, 1942

*Ambulance Plunges Bringing Death to Two, August 24, 1943*

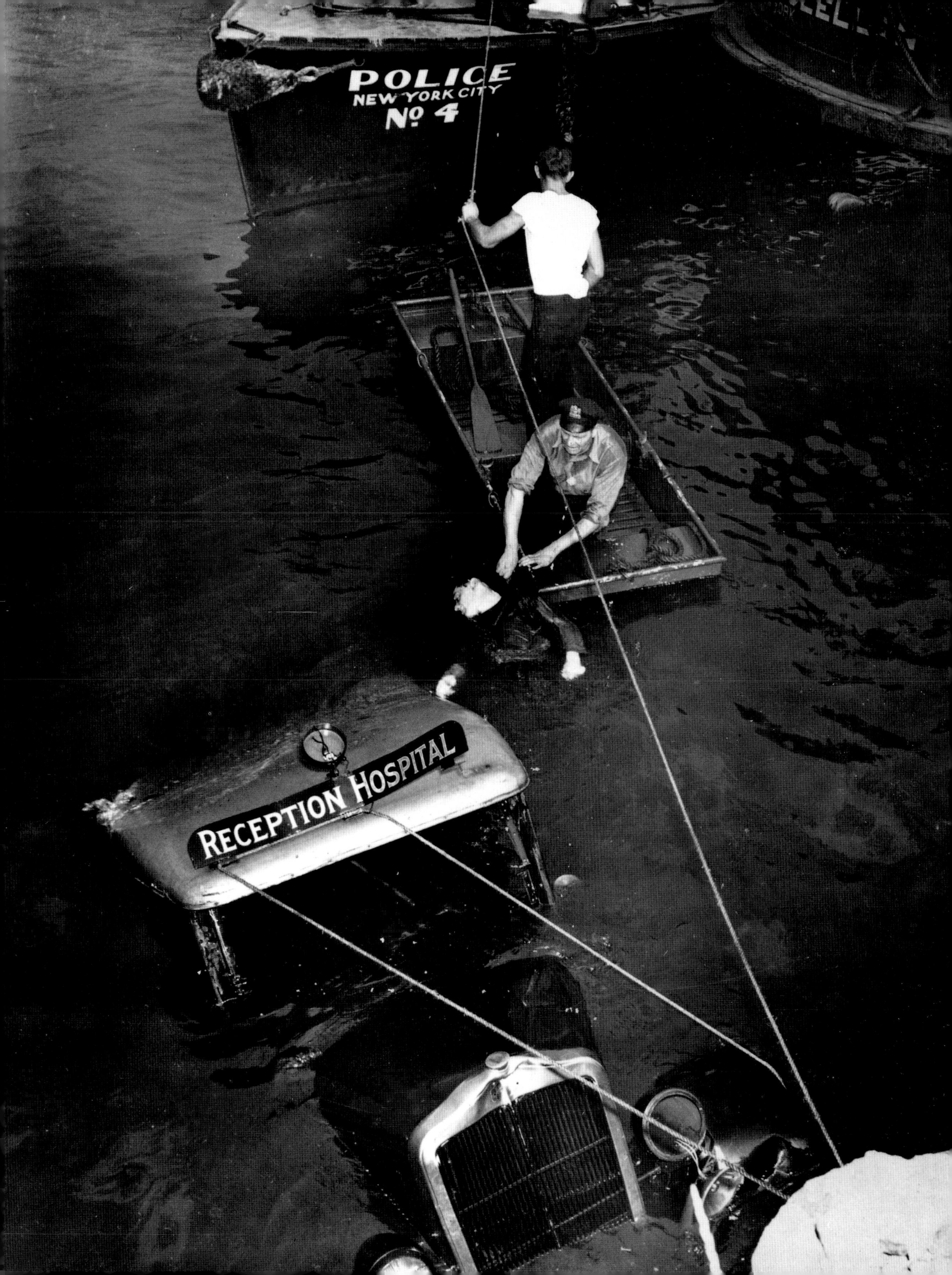
POLICE
NEW YORK CITY
Nº 4
RECEPTION HOSPITAL

*Cab Crash,* c. 1941

*Car Crash Upper Fifth Ave., July 13, 1941*

"Death Strikes a Truck Driver at Dawn," September 7, 1944

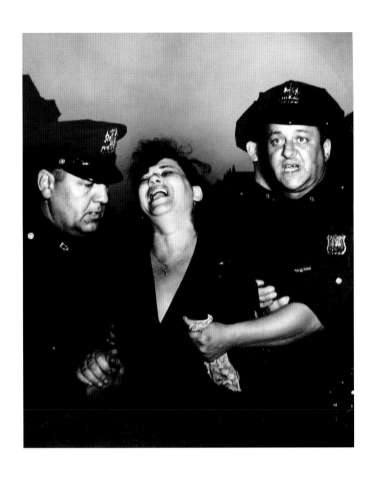

"... And the Living Suffer," *Mrs. Vanta Supik, Wife of the Dead Truck Driver*, September 7, 1944

"Sudden Death for One... Sudden Shock for the Other." *Mrs. Dorothy Reportella,
Accused of Hitting Bread Truck with Her Car*, September 7, 1944

*Victim of Auto Accident, October 29, 1939*

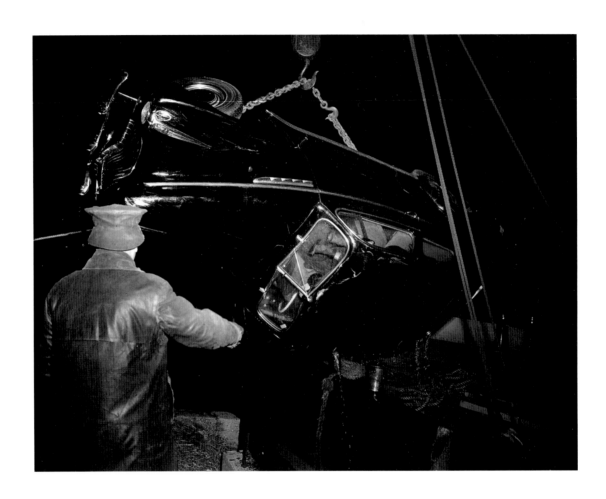

"Out of the River," February 24, 1942

*Accident on Grand Central Station Roof, 1944*

"The dead lay still...," August 18, 1941

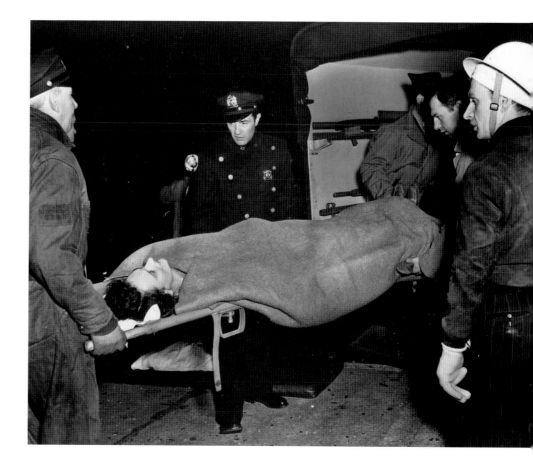

"The Human Cop," 1943

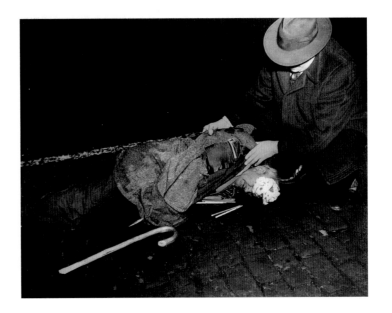

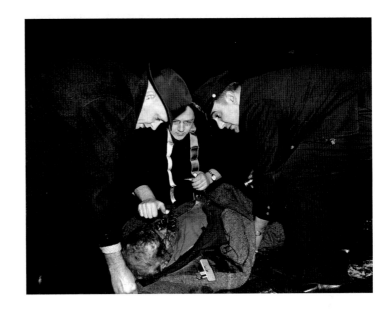

*Frank Birskowsky, on Sidewalk
of the Bowery,* December 28, 1942

"Hit by Taxi," December 28, 1942

"Last Rites," December 28, 1942

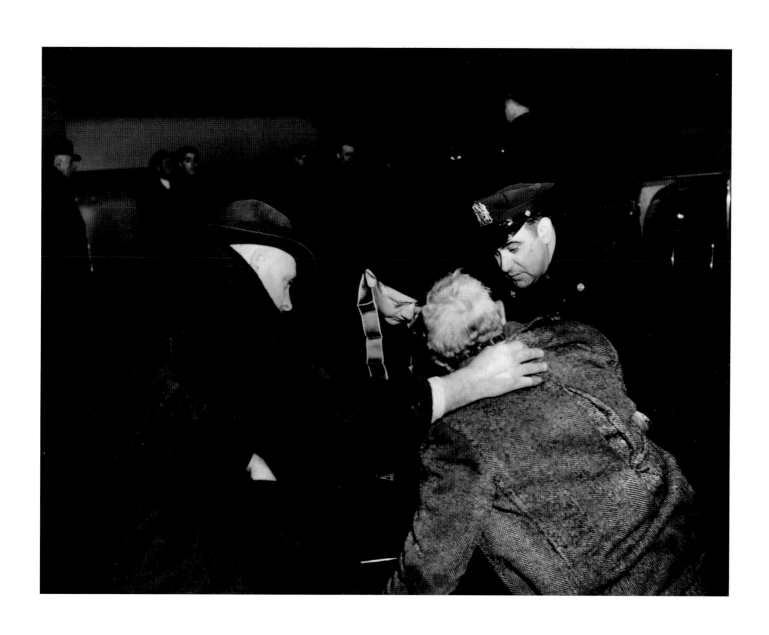

"Comforted by Police," December 28, 1942

"Night Duty," July 20, 1941

*Bringing Home the Bird,* December, 1943

*This Young Boy Got His Hand Caught in the Cup Machine,* c. 1942

"Simply Add Boiling Water," 1937

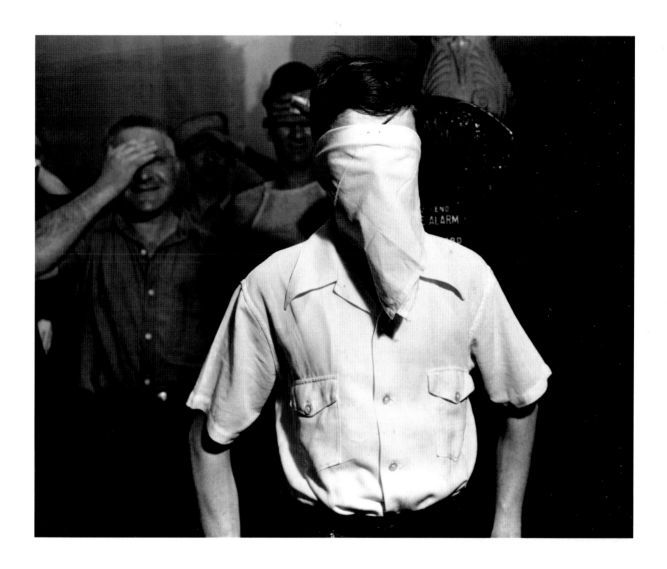

*Man covering face from smoke, c.1943*

"A couple driven out from the burning tenement...," April 23, 1944

"I Cried When I Took This Picture," *Mrs. Henrietta Torres and Her Daughter Ada watch as Another Daughter and Her Son Die in Fire*, December 15, 1939

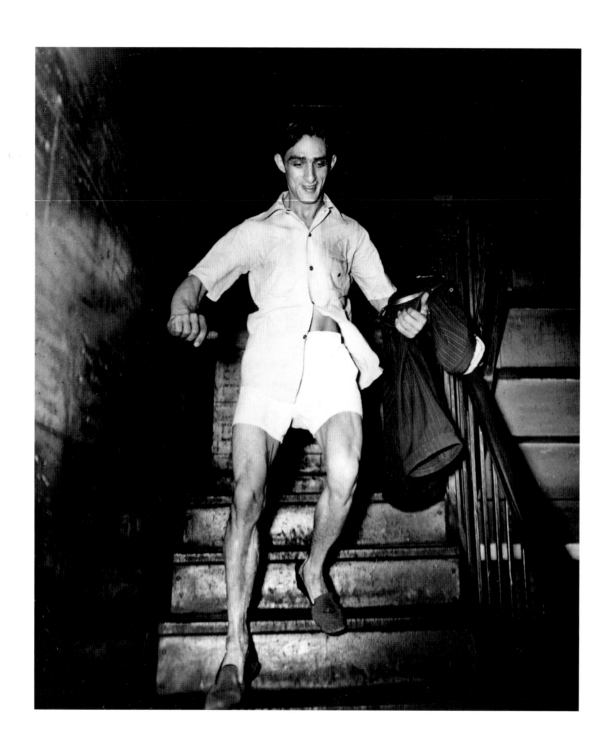

"What to Wear," October 15, 1941

*Elderly Woman Rescued from Fire at*
*209 West 62nd St., July 20, 1940*

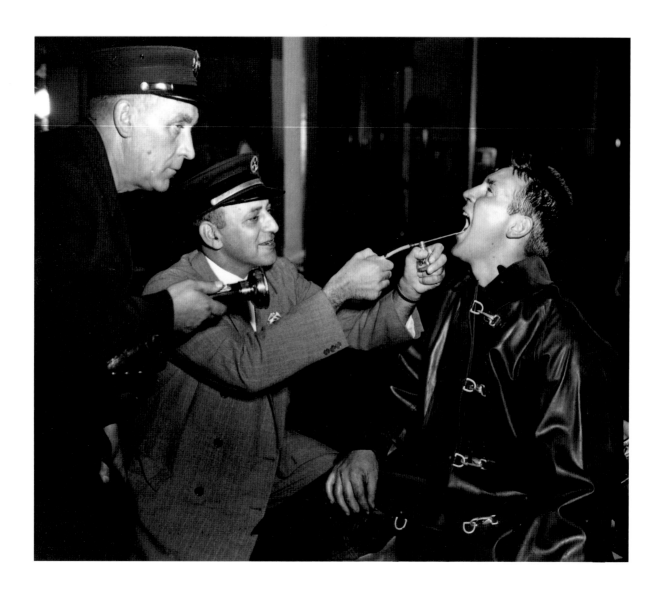

*Two-Alarm Blaze that Knocked Out 36 Firemen, September 2, 1941*

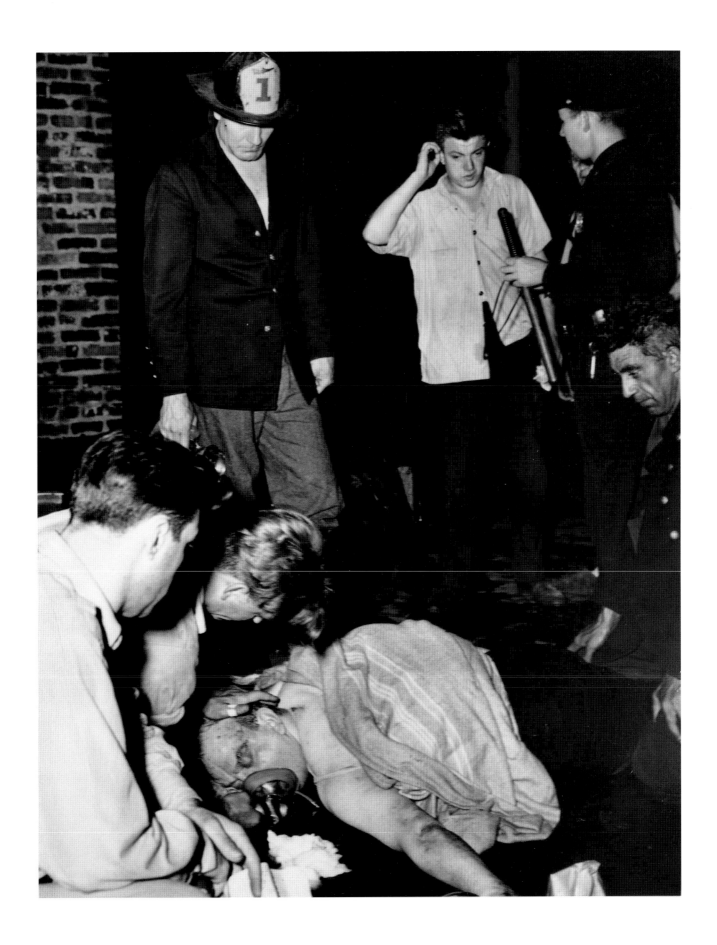

*Ten Firemen Overcome in Washington Street Market Blaze, May 19, 1941*

"Two Firemen Rescuing Angel," 1939

"Someone Rushed in and Saved the Holy Scrolls from the Synagogue," March 2, 1943

*Fire Lieutenant Vincent Burns Rescues Mrs. Carl Taylor from a Fire at 136 W. 64th St., January 13, 1941*

*Henry Geller, Weeps Over Loss of His Tobacco Shop, July 28, 1941*

*Brooklyn Mattress Factory Burned, February 1, 1942*

*Norma Devine is Sammy's Mae West*, December 4, 1944

"Sammy's on the Bowery," December, 1944

*Tilly Schneider — songs sweet and low*, December 4, 1944

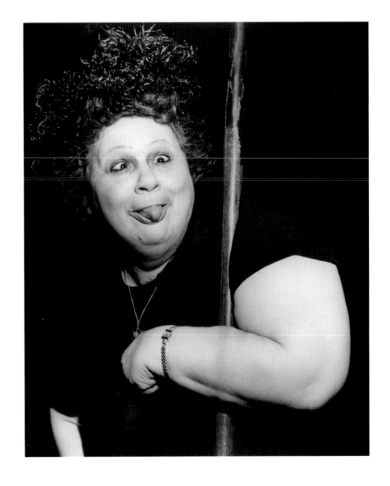

*Monty Reed,* "Master of Ceremonies," December 4, 1944

*Daisy Lewis, Entertainer,* January 16, 1944

*Billie Dauscha (left) and Mabel Sidney (right), Bowery Entertainers, December 4, 1944*

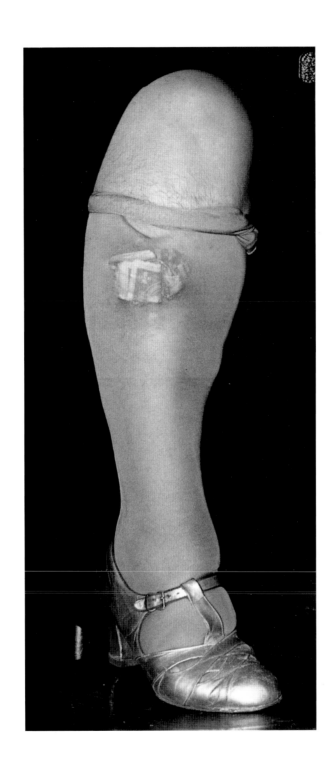

"The Bowery Saving's Bank," December 4, 1944

"After the Opera... at Sammy's Night Club on the Bowery," c. 1944

"Blond woman, after the Opera... at Sammy's Night Club on the Bowery," c. 1944

"Sophisticated Lady," c. 1943

"Sammy and Guests," c. 1943

"New Year's at 5 in the morning in a night club, I found this 3 year old
with his parents welcoming in the New Year with milk," 1943

*Hot dog vendor at Sammy's Bar, c. 1943*

"Shorty, the Bowery Cherub, New Year's
Eve at Sammy's Bar," 1943

"Crowd at Coney Island, Temperature 89 degrees... They came early, and stayed late," July 22, 1940

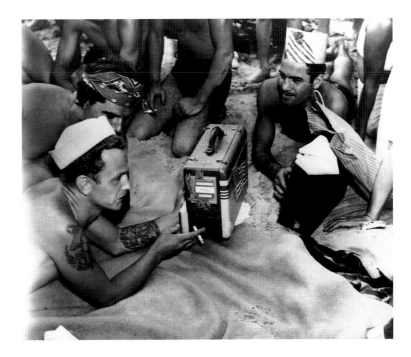

*First Aid for Ripped Slacks*, June 9, 1941
"A Stitch in Time"

*During the War*, c. 1944

"Lovers at Coney Island," c. 1943 [Infrared Negative]

"Girl on Life Guard Station," c. 1940 [Infrared Negative]

"Lovers on the Sand," c. 1943 [Infrared Negative]

*Sunbathing*, January 20, 1941

"Lost Children," June 9, 1941

*Spring Sunbathers,* March 24, 1941

SHOWERS

*Spring Comes to Coney Island,* March 24, 1941     147

## Picturing New York, the Naked City:
## Weegee and Urban Photography     Ellen Handy

*When you find yourself beginning to feel a bond between yourself and the people you photograph, when you laugh and cry with their laughter and tears, you will know you are on the right track.*

Weegee, "Camera Tips"[1]

*"I must go and find out," I said, "what is the Voice of this City. Other cities have voices. It is an assignment. I must have it. New York," I continued, in a rising tone, "had better not hand me a cigar and say: 'Old man, I can't talk for publication.' No other city acts in that way. Chicago says, unhesitatingly, 'I will;' Philadelphia says, 'I should;' New Orleans says, 'I used to;' Louisville says, 'Don't care if I do;' St. Louis says, 'Excuse me;' Pittsburgh says, 'Smoke up.' Now, New York — " ...*

O. Henry, "The Voice of the City"[2]

A hard-bitten tabloid news photographer, aficionado of the New York City underworld, and urban storyteller *par excellence*, Weegee was also a modern master of the art of photography. He didn't invent tabloid news photography, but he perfected it, making it possible for the first time for pictures to function both as grainy, newsprint attention-grabbers and as sophisticated compositions worthy of museum walls. Weegee was above all a professional — and an artist. Not only was he a superb press photographer, he was also an experimental filmmaker, abstract photographer, poet of the everyday, and writer of no little talent. The bold, graphic, instantly legible style of his work and its gritty, often disturbing subject matter are both characteristically urban. Weegee belongs to the long line of urban documentary photographers whose work is so disparate that it scarcely constitutes a genre. Energetically creating his own legend and shamelessly promoting himself whenever possible, Weegee became a larger-than-life figure in the life of the city as well as in the history of photography. He created a vision of the city as a place that contained gangsters, cheerful laborers, down-and-outers, victims of violence or tragedy, pleasure-seekers, endless spectacles and their audiences — and characters like himself.

Working primarily for the once-numerous daily newspapers of New York City, Weegee compiled a unique and compelling body of work during the 1930s, 1940s, and 1950s, which he called "the famous pictures of a violent era, the pictures that all the great papers with all their resources couldn't get, and had to buy from me." He added that "in shooting these pictures, I had also photographed the soul of the city I knew and loved."[3] The work he collected in his first book, *Naked City* (1945), is among his finest. That volume expresses the quintessence of Weegee's work: his recognition that a city is a repository of stories, that the many millions who comprise its population are players on its stage. Its open-hearted dedication reads, "TO YOU THE PEOPLE OF NEW YORK." Weegee is one of those artists who are inextricably associated with a single place. Despite his birth in Lemberg (Lvov), in what is now Ukraine, and his subsequent work in Europe and Hollywood, Weegee is *the* New York City photographer.

Weegee's work can be considered as covering the territory that falls between two remarkable images published in *Naked City*. The first is the book's frontispiece: a view of the city's skyline illuminated by a lurid flash of lightning (1940). Aside from this image, the celebrated skyscrapers of Manhattan are all but invisible in

1. Weegee, "Camera Tips," in Naked City (1945), reprinted New York: Da Capo Press, 1973, p. 243.

2. O. Henry [William Sydney Porter], "The Voice of the City," in The Voice of the City, New York: Doubleday, Page and Company, 1908, p. 5.

3. Weegee by Weegee: An Autobiography, New York: Ziff-Davis Publishing Company, 1961, p. 76.

*Striking Beauty,* July 29, 1940

Weegee's work. His sensibility was precisely the opposite of that expressed in popular New York films like *On the Town* (1949), in which a group of happy sailors from out of town go on a spree in the Big Apple, singing:

> New York, New York, It's a wonderful town
> The Bronx is up and the Battery is down
> The people ride in a hole in the ground
> New York, New York—It's a wonderful town.[4]

Weegee emphatically eschewed picture postcard views and tourist attractions as photographic subjects. But this image of the city transfixed, energized, and dazzled by a cosmic flash is actually a pun. The lightning stands in for the characteristic flash of artificial light Weegee used to reveal his subjects in the city's darkness—in this photograph, nature imitates art, or at least Weegee. That light-soaked quality, resultant from the high-wattage flashgun Weegee used with his Speed Graphic 4 × 5 inch camera, is an essential component of his style.[5]

Weegee's work is defined by searing chiaroscuro. His preference for working at night, the glaring lighting of the city streets, and the particularly inky darkness of New York nights all contribute to the intense tonal contrast in his work. The prevailing darkness of so many of his images is as expressive as that employed by such artists as Goya, Rembrandt, and Edward Hopper in their graphic works. It is so prominent in "Car Crash Upper Fifth Ave." (1941), for instance, that darkness acts as a vivid framing device, calling attention to the victims of the crash (page 105).

The second of these two emblematic photographs from *Naked City* depicts the record stub of a thirty-five-dollar check Weegee received in payment for a pair of photographs submitted to Time, Inc. The accountant's memo on the check stub reads "TWO MURDERS." A print of this image is prominently displayed in a self-portrait of the artist at home, tacked to the impromptu bulletin board he made of the wall over his bed.[6] The witty and ironic translation of Weegee's graphic crime photography into this concise and reductive format is virtually Duchampian. The

4. On the Town, *directed by Gene Kelly and Stanley Donen, released by MGM, 1949, songs by Betty Comden and Adolph Green.*

5. *Weegee's artistry with the flash and its dramatic effects upon the look of his work have been most effectively described by John Coplans in his article "Weegee the Famous," in* Art in America, *vol. 65, no. 5 (September-October 1977), pp. 37-41.*

6. *The self-portrait in which this photograph appears is reproduced in a section of plates in* Weegee by Weegee, *np.*

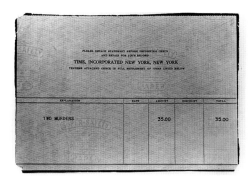

"Check for Two Murders," c. 1939

7. The increasing institutionalization of fine art photography during these years is traced in a seminal article by Christopher Phillips, "The Judgment Seat of Photography" (see October 22 Fall 1982), which recounts the changing practices of the Museum of Modern Art's Photography Department. This account identifies the fluctuations in the museum's position regarding the autonomy of fine art photography, and thus indirectly casts an interesting light on the otherwise surprising fact that Weegee's work was exhibited at MoMA, despite his distinctly nonartistic credentials.

8. (Brassaï) Paris de nuit, Paris: Art et Métier Graphique, 1933. The connection between Brassaï and Weegee's work was most eloquently argued by Colin L. Westerbeck, Jr., in an article entitled "Night Light: Brassaï and Weegee," in Artforum, vol. 15, no. 4 (December 1976), pp. 34-45.

9. Weegee by Weegee, p. 33.

10. Bill Brandt, The English at Home, London: Batsford, 1936, and A Night in London, London: Country Life, 1938.

11. August Sander, Anlitz der Zeit, Munich: Transmare, 1929.

image's insistence upon the commercial function of his work and its negotiability in the free market of images is an important aspect of Weegee's work. Few previous photographers have called attention so deliberately to their own roles as authors and producers of imagery, to the economic basis of their production, and to the circulation of images in the larger economy. This self-consciousness and a willingness to make images that incorporate his own presence on the scene directly relate to Weegee's situation at the intersection of photographic mass media and of fine art photography during a period when those aspects of the medium diverged radically in the wake of earlier twentieth-century modernism's experiments.[7]

At once professional photojournalist for the tabloids and artist-auteur, Weegee was anomalous in his insistence upon conjoining what other photographers of the time most deliberately sought to separate. Just as photography began to be taught in art schools and exhibited in museums, and when the work of purist fine art photographers such as Ansel Adams, Edward Weston, and Harry Callahan began to command respect from museums, collectors, and historians and to symbolize the separation of fine art and commercial work, Weegee harked back to an earlier chapter in the history of modernism. Like the Bauhaus and Constructivist artists who designed useful artworks as well as beautiful objects of utility, Weegee found no conflict between presenting his attention-getting crime photos both as news images for the masses and as artistic camera-studies. Endorsing the democracy of photography as a modernist medium is a position more typically European than American, and indeed, Weegee's work is in some ways closer in spirit to that of Europeans like Brassaï and Bill Brandt or even August Sander than it is to that of his American contemporaries.

Brassaï's book Paris de nuit (Paris at Night), like Weegee's work, displays a fascination with the demi-mondaine and its nocturnal pursuit of sex, pleasure, and crime, which Brassaï used to represent the whole of Parisian life.[8] But Weegee's embrace of New York is more comprehensive and less decadent than Brassaï's tour of brothels, cafés, and street gang territories. In speaking of just one neighborhood of New York, the Lower East Side, Weegee recalled the range and diversity of its amenities, including the "Grand Street Playhouse, Henry Street Settlement House, Educational Alliance, music schools, synagogues, and whorehouses. I liked them and attended them all."[9] The urban matrix was essential to Weegee's working method, and equally essential as an ingredient in his process of self-fashioning. He created himself out of the raw materials of the city he portrayed.

Brandt's books The English at Home and A Night in London are more varied than Brassaï's in their portrayal of the minutiae of social class, and in this they more closely resemble Weegee's Naked City.[10] If Brassaï and Brandt analyzed their respective cities as artistic sociologists with a taste of Surrealism in their makeup, Sander was far more methodical and directly documentary in his intentions. His photographic inventory of the German people was a typological study organized around the abstract categories of race, class, and profession rather than urban location.[11] What Sander and Weegee share is an interest in the typical rather than the remarkable as photographic subject. But while Sander isolated his subjects from the narrative flow of their lives, Weegee sought out context and drama. His collective portrait of the city marks it as a place of infinite stories.

The emphasis upon narrative and subject matter is also the point of greatest distinction between Weegee and Bauhaus or Constructivist artists. Of the latter, however, Weegee's sensibility most nearly parallels that of László Moholy-Nagy and

Paul Strand, *Blind Woman*, New York, 1916

12. *László Moholy-Nagy*, Malerei, Fotographie, Film, *Munich: Langen, 1925.*

13. Weegee by Weegee p. 36.

14. Weegee by Weegee p. 37.

Alexander Rodchenko. Moholy-Nagy appreciated news photography, and reproduced it in his celebrated treatise *Malerei, Fotographie, Film* (Painting, Photography, Film), but his own photographs were typically modernist abstractions very unlike Weegee's work.[12] Rodchenko's abstractive elevated views looking downward upon the parades of Young Pioneers marching through the streets contrast strikingly with Weegee's searing "Their First Murder" (1941; page 64), in which a horde of children dashes toward the murder scene and toward the camera, with responses ranging from horror to unholy glee to passionate intensity. The picture both shares and records with alarm the intensity of human fascination with violence. Weegee was always honest about his stake in the tabloid photographer's stock in trade: crime. As he put it, "Crime was my oyster, and I liked it … my post-graduate course in life and photography."[13]

Weegee's tabloid-oriented subject matter differentiates his work from that of most of the other great documentary photographers. Urban survey work is so diverse in purpose, scope, and style that it constitutes not one tradition, but many. These include primarily architectural surveys like those of Charles Marville and Eugène Atget, ethnographic studies like those of John Thomson, August Sander, Brassaï, and Brandt, and of course the work of muckraking crusaders like Jacob Riis and Lewis Hine. A colder, more elegant and formal eye was turned upon the city by artists like Paul Strand, Charles Sheeler, Walker Evans, Berenice Abbott, and Moholy-Nagy, while Lisette Model, Helen Levitt, and Sid Grossman each identified specific aspects of the city and its denizens as sufficient subject matter for their work, rather than struggling to embrace every aspect of urban life. But unlike these predecessors and contemporaries, Weegee's peculiar style was shaped by his market, which demanded endless slight variations on a handful of themes. As he described it, "There had to be a good meaty story to get the editors to buy the pictures. A truck crash with the driver trapped inside, his face a crisscross of blood … a tenement-house fire with the screaming people being carried down the aerial ladder clutching their babies, dogs, cats, canaries, parrots, monkeys, and even snakes … a just-shot gangster, lying in the gutter, well-dressed in his dark suit and pearl hat, hot off the griddle, with a priest, who seemed to appear from nowhere, giving him the last rites … just-caught stick-up men, lady burglars, etc." [14]

The photographs of fires provide some of the most consistently serial iconography in Weegee's work. Anxious survivors on the street outside burning buildings clutch objects they've managed to save, and which differentiate them from each other as do the attributes held by saints in old master paintings. Weegee encompasses both the sacred and the profane: an old man grasps a few items of clothing in bewilderment (1944), while in another picture, a young, open-mouthed man embraces the Torah scrolls saved from a synagogue fire (1943). In numerous pictures of corpses on city streets, Weegee's mood ranges from grim darkness to the startling humor evidenced in pictures like "Mail Early for Delivery Before Christmas" (1940) and "Joy of Living" (1942), where nearby items of street furniture are drafted to provide ironic commentary on the murdered bodies below.

Unlike Brassaï's Paris, Weegee's New York is not an ecstatic city. Unlike Brandt's London, it is not segregated by social class. And unlike Rodchenko's Moscow, it is not purely a stage set in which life assumes the form of modernist abstraction. Rather, it is a dark place sometimes illuminated by flashes of joy and warmed by unexpected manifestations of human kindness. It is a city of high adrenaline, rhythmic motion, and frequent surprises. It is a city of a type that was new when

Weegee discovered and helped to invent it in the 1940s. It has since become so familiar, however, that we need to make some effort to apprehend the innovation of this urban vision.

The city's inherent qualities are a mix of folly and pleasure, glamour and low-life dangers, high society and huddled masses. The city was at once the continent's capital of high finance and of fine art. Jackson Pollock was forming his style, Cole Porter was turning out popular tunes, and *New Yorker* magazine writers like Joseph Mitchell and A. J. Liebling were honing their prose, all in the same mad, passionate city surveyed by Weegee.[15] The exuberance and unlikely subject matter of many of Weegee's photographs constitute a hymn of praise to the city's human diversity. He photographed scenes as disparate as the mingling of society matrons and show girls, a women's art class sketching a scantily clad male model, a lady cab driver and the inflating giant balloons of the annual Macy's Thanksgiving Day parade, a giraffe spending the night in an improvised dormitory, a man chasing a turkey, and a smiling cop holding some outsize women's underpants.

Weegee's New York looks back to the hard-drinking sophistication of the 1920s and 1930s, but glimpses of the 1950s and 1960s appear in his work as well — for instance, he made portraits of both Andy Warhol and Marilyn Monroe. The New York City of the 1940s was the prosperous heir to the glamour of the Roaring Twenties, which left memories of hot jazz, great silent moving pictures, writers like F. Scott Fitzgerald, and humorists like Dorothy Parker and Robert Benchley. But 1940s New York was also on the cusp of what were to be its subsequent adventures, such as the emergence of the New York School painters and the Actor's Studio circle, the shenanigans of the Beats, and the party scene at Warhol's Factory. Weegee's New York overlapped wonderfully and surprisingly with that of many other celebrated artists, writers, and musicians. It is to this larger world of modern urban culture, much more than to the history of documentary photography, that he belongs.

Of all those who have shaped Manhattan's chaotic vitality into coherent images of "New York life," only one comes close to matching Weegee for energy and empathy, apparent omniscience and humor: the great short story writer, O. Henry.[16] This comparison of a writer and a photographer is particularly appropriate because Weegee's photographs are in themselves stories, as tautly compressed, unexpected, and full of good punch lines as any of O. Henry's classic tales of life in the city he called "Baghdad-by-the-Subway." The title of one of his books, *The Voice of the City*, could have served equally well for a book by Weegee.[17] Like Weegee, O. Henry invented a pseudonym for himself, and then developed a corresponding artistic persona. The two shared many subjects: Coney Island outings, street fights, down-and-outers sleeping on park benches, drunks in neighborhood bars, high society types going slumming. Weegee himself was just the kind of character whose adventures O. Henry would have loved to chronicle, and O. Henry (who started writing his New York stories while an inmate in jail) was just the type to appear in a photo by Weegee. Both were romantic realists, passionate about recording the urban experience, and willing to play upon the whole spectrum of human emotions. As Weegee wrote about his work for a brief period as a violin accompanist in a silent movie theater: "I loved playing on the emotions of the audience as they watched the silent movies. I could move them to either happiness or sorrow. I had all the standard selections for any situation. I suppose that my fiddle-playing was a subconscious kind of training for my future in photography." [18]

15. *Joseph Mitchell spent the greater part of his journalistic career roving the city, locating characters and writing about them. He wrote a profile of Weegee, and Weegee returned the favor. (Weegee by Weegee, p. 85.) His writings were originally published in the* New Yorker, *and later collected as several books (*McSorley's Wonderful Saloon, *1943;* Old Mr. Flood, *1948;* The Bottom of the Harbor, *1960;* Joe Gould's Secret, *1965; all of which were reprinted as* Up in the Old Hotel, *New York: Vintage Books, 1992).*

*A. J. Liebling, another journalistic lover of eccentric New York City types, specialized in character studies of people on the streets and in lowbrow public life. His mastery of dialogue creates effects as vivid and authentic as the gestures and moments Weegee captured in his photographs. After first publication in the* New Yorker, *many of Liebling's pieces were collected in* Back Where I Came From *(1938), reprinted San Francisco: North Point Press, 1989.*

16. *O. Henry's democratic view of what constituted subject matter in the vast tumult of New York life was very close to that held by Weegee. As an introduction to his collection of stories* The Four Million *(New York: Doubleday, Page and Company, 1906), O. Henry wrote: "Not long ago someone invented the assertion that there were only 'Four Hundred' people in New York City who were really worth noticing. But a wiser man has arisen—the census taker—and his larger estimate of human interest has been favored in marking out the field of interest of these little stories of the 'Four Million.'"*

17. *O. Henry,* The Voice of the City, *1908.*

18. *Weegee by Weegee, p. 27.*

In Weegee's work, it is seldom that a single emotion is conveyed by a picture, and the emotions depicted are not necessarily identical to those the viewer is directed to feel. The power of many of his images derives from the disparity between what their subjects feel or express, and the reaction of the viewer. "Life Saving Attempt" (1940) is one of the most finely honed of Weegee's numerous audience-reaction studies. A knot of stooping figures around the prostrate victim includes busy medics, visibly worried onlookers, and a young girl in a bathing suit. Upon catching sight of Weegee, she reflexively but incongruously smiled broadly for the camera. In his greatest photograph, "The Critic" (1943; page 172), two of the picture's subjects express self-satisfaction, and the third derision. The picture's fierce humor derives from its mix of rage, irony, and complacency, and from its ability to make the viewer register far more and different emotions than the people portrayed. The jeering woman at the right serves as a surrogate for the anger Weegee felt but didn't express directly, and thus the picture operates (as all satires do) simultaneously as humor and critique.

Although his work is strongly narrative, Weegee created very few picture story sequences. Most often, the whole story is told or implied by a single shot. One important exception to this is Weegee's multipicture exploration of a performance by Frank Sinatra (1944; page 207), a string of pictures of ecstatic female fans at a concert which appears in Naked City.[19] Their frenzy is an antecedent to the next generation's Beatlemania, and the grouping of pictures explores the workings of the culture industry. Weegee shrewdly assessed this phenomenon as akin to his own production of images for the masses — and did so with perhaps a slight envy of the acclaim and attention commanded by the live performer as opposed to the lone photographer. Regardless, Weegee's scrutiny of the young fans' entirely unguarded responses resulted in pictures of great intimacy.

Intimacy is precisely what makes New York City intolerable and sublime by turns. Weegee's work depicts this with a thousand variations, particularly in relation to the ways in which the crowded city makes intimates of strangers through the abrupt overlapping of their zones of personal space in the public realm. Sleepers on park benches, lovers embracing on public beaches at night, and people in crowds of all kinds were perfect subjects for Weegee. Such intimacy is touchingly displayed in "Heat Spell" (1941; page 46), a picture both tender and voyeuristic, and one which reveals a paradox familiar to most photographers: Weegee gets closer to his subjects when they don't know he's there, as in his many images of sleepers. His affectionate image of the children curled up together on the fire escape like a litter of kittens is the work of someone who had himself known the experience of impromptu urban camping as a young slum-dweller.

Weegee's own intimate connection with his subjects could derive from empathy as well as familiarity, as in his photograph of two shawl-clad weeping women (page 121), who are as tragic and grief-wrenched as any of the figures in Picasso's Guernica. In Naked City, he captioned this picture (1939) as follows: "I Cried When I Took This Picture. Mother and daughter cry and look hopelessly up as another daughter and her young baby are burning to death in the top floor of the tenement . . . firemen couldn't reach them in time . . . on account of the stairway collapsing."[20]

The instantaneity and emotional immediacy of this scene, and the photographer's frank avowal of his own response, are characteristic. How different this image is from the urban portraiture practiced by Paul Strand in photographs like "Blind Woman" (1916). Strand's photograph is powerful and uncomfortable for viewers

19. Weegee's photographs of Sinatra and his fans comprise chapter 8, "Frankie," of Naked City, pp. 112-23.

20. Naked City, p. 74.

who, through his extreme close-up, find themselves face to face with a subject who can't look back at the photographer. The vehement-looking blind woman wears a sign reading "BLIND" slung around her neck, and her sightless eyes skew abruptly sideways. The slow deliberation of Strand's composition is neither more nor less intrusive upon its subject than Weegee's rapidly made flash photograph. But Weegee's identification with the sorrow of the two women he photographed means that he played a more explicit role in this photograph than the more reticent Strand did in his picture.

One of the great pleasures of Weegee's work is his occasional recognition of innocence in tough times and places. But he also regularly displayed considerable cynicism, and sought out instances of all that is contrary to innocence. His photograph of a beaming boy holding a sign reading "Down with the Japs" at a street demonstration (1942; page 180) suggests that a gleeful savagery lies not far below the surface of children and adults. His work is sometimes similar to Helen Levitt's in this way. Her pictures of children in wild, uninhibited, and unidealized activities have an immediacy and authenticity that Weegee would have envied, with a delicacy of psychological nuance very different from his work.[21]

Whether cynic, seeker of innocence, or romantic, ultimately Weegee was solidly a humanist, and his New York is a seething mass of individuals with emotions, dreams, problems, and stories. It differs in every way from the gleaming, depopulated, cubistic site portrayed by Precisionist photographers like Charles Sheeler.[22] For those artists, as for Walker Evans, Berenice Abbott, and Ralph Steiner, the city was a place composed primarily of architecture. For Weegee, it was an event, composed of people, and buildings were not large-scale sculptures ornamenting the skyline but rather containers for myriad human experiences. In Weegee's series of photographs of 60 Wall Street Tower, he gave individual identities to the thronging crowds populating one skyscraper, including a solitary cleaning lady at work late at night, almost lost in the darkness of the emptying building (1940).[23]

Restlessness and wonder are equally important qualities in Weegee's work, one producing the other. Weegee was certainly not alone in prowling the city — its literary and artistic histories include entries about fellow night-crawlers. Perhaps the most surprising and interesting parallel is between Weegee and Alfred Stieglitz. Both photographers were ardent New Yorkers from Jewish families recently settled in the new world, the Stieglitz family from Germany, and the Felligs (Weegee's family name) from Galicia. Both men frequently photographed at night under technically difficult conditions. Both relied with unusual intensity upon photography to make and express their emotional connection to the world, and both men produced serial bodies of work.[24] Their more evident differences can be expressed as a series of oppositions: frankly commercial tabloid work vs. high art; the artist as a member of the working class, identified with criminals and the unemployed, vs. the artist as a member of the leisure class; unlimited reproducible images vs. unique prints; a mass audience vs. an elite audience; immersion in the city vs. alienation from the city; humor and shock tactics vs. exaltation.

Both Weegee and Stieglitz were seekers after invisible things in the darkness of the city. Stieglitz was looking for manifestations of his own soul, while Weegee was attempting to photograph what was about to happen. Stieglitz paced the streets, wrapped in a long cape, solitary and contemplative, while Weegee cruised through the sleeping city in his 1938 Chevrolet, racing to the scene of any event that might be a picture in the making. His uncanny instinct about where news events would

21. Such pictures appear in Helen Levitt's classic book A Way of Seeing (1965), reprinted Durham, NC: Duke University Press, 1989, p. 59.

22. Precisionist and abstractive modernist photographic rendering of the city is discussed at greater length in Ellen Handy's essay "The Idea and the Fact: Painting, Photography, Film, Precisionists, and the Real World," in Gail Stavitsky's book, Precisionism in America 1915-1941: Reordering Reality, New York: Harry N. Abrams, Inc., 1994.

23. The 60 Wall Street Tower series of photographs appears in Weegee's People (1946), reprinted New York: Da Capo Press, 1975, np.

24. Stieglitz wrote about his symbolist/expressionist theory of photography in 1923 in a brief essay entitled "How I Came to Photograph Clouds," published in the The Amateur Photographer and Photography, vol. 56, no. 1819, p. 255. Rosalind Krauss has explored this theme in an article titled "Alfred Stieglitz's 'Equivalents,'" Arts Magazine, February 1980, pp. 134-37. The topic has also been thoughtfully discussed by Sarah Greenough, "How Stieglitz Came to Photograph Clouds," in Peter Walch and Thomas Barrow, eds., Perspectives on Photography, Essays in Honor of Beaumont Newhall, Albuquerque: University of New Mexico Press, 1986.

occur led to his sobriquet, Weegee, after the Ouija board, whose powers of divination he seemed to share. He often made extravagant, implausible claims about his own prescience, just as Stieglitz did about his ability to express his emotions through photographs. Both men harnessed their psychic aspirations to photographic practice. Unlike Stieglitz, whose portrait photographs required lengthy, intimate sittings, during which Stieglitz compelled the attention of his subjects absolutely, Weegee often photographed unobtrusively. Some of his images were taken by stealth, with the tact of invisibility, achieved by means of infrared film that allowed him to work in darkness without a visible flash.

Stieglitz's photograph "The Terminal" (1893) shows a team of steaming draft horses straining to pull a trolley car around a pivot at the end of the line before beginning the weary return journey on a snowy day. It emphasizes the deadening qualities of work, and renders the city as a place of labor. Weegee's photograph of an old vegetable peddler (1944) is a somewhat closer view of a single horse plodding through snow and darkness led by a bearded old man. Side by side, man and beast are cold and weary but sturdy and persevering. They face the camera and advance upon it. Stieglitz's picture, less intimate and more complex in structure, puts the man leading the horses at the center of the composition, but with his back to the camera, his face unseen and his individuality effaced. Weegee's emotional connection with his subjects and Stieglitz's alienation and use of his subjects for metaphorical ends are apparent in this pair of pictures.

The juxtaposition of the utterly disparate Stieglitz and Weegee would be a purely fanciful one in any city other than New York, where sooner or later practically everyone rubs shoulders with everyone else. Weegee made it his business to seek out the frail, aging Stieglitz at his last gallery, An American Place. Weegee's account of their meeting is poignant, and the authenticity of his tale is confirmed by the photograph he took of Stieglitz (1944), slumped on his cot in the back room of the gallery. It is one of the finest portraits ever taken of that domineering and compelling man.

"Alfred Stieglitz," wrote Weegee in *Naked City,* "became famous both in Europe and America as the master of the camera, and what did his fame get him?...There was a smell of disinfectant like in a sick room....Stieglitz pointed to the phone near the cot...'It never rings...I have been deserted.'...He hadn't made a photograph for the past ten years...had never used the products of one company, because they had advertised, 'You push the button. We'll do the rest.'...That slogan was a bad influence on photographers because a picture needed careful planning and thinking and could only be captured on film at a certain fleeting fraction of a second...and once that passed, that fraction of time was dead and could never be brought back to life again....He had never compromised with his photography, for money or to please an editor. One had to be free to do creative work....Suddenly he slumped over in pain. 'My heart, it's bad,' he said in a whisper as he slumped over on the cot. I waited till he recovered then left quietly ... wondering if that elusive fame I was after was worthwhile."[25]

If Stieglitz's New York was the city of ambition (as he titled one view of the towers of lower Manhattan) and a diagram of his soul, Weegee's New York was purely a corporeal city. It was substantial, enduring, vivid, and full of people with physical sensations and desires. Tired feet, crude humor, bulging flesh, sweaty or smelly bodies are not excluded from Weegee's city. Blood, pain, and other highly physical realities appear or are intimated in his photographs.

25. Naked City, pp. 233-35.

Alfred Stieglitz  *The Terminal,* c. 1892-3

*Incident in the Snowstorm,* December 28, 1944

26. *This image appears in* Naked City *on page 218. On the facing page is a photograph of a crying foundling baby who seems distinctly less pampered.*

27. *O. Henry, "Man About Town," in* The Four Million.

In Weegee's photographs, but not Stieglitz's, New York was an emphatically classed city. "The Critic" is a piece of withering social commentary which equated bedizened socialites attending the opera with the unkempt bag lady watching their arrival, and satirized each in an instant's exposure. But Weegee's deeply ingrained awareness of class pops up in less likely places as well. His *Naked City* caption for the picture of a handsome black poodle (1940) reads: "This is a high class pooch . . . you see them on Park Avenue, Fifth Avenue, Central Park West, on streets where the better classes live. . . . Well fed, well trimmed and house broken. . . except on the public streets."[26]

Collectively, Weegee's work makes a strong refutation of the great national myth of America as a classless, egalitarian society. As an immigrant from Europe to New York's crowded Lower East Side, Weegee grew up without time to absorb the small-town doctrines that by the 1940s had become defining elements of American life. But if he was too observant of social realities to make a quintessential American, he was even further from being a European-style *flaneur.* The birth of modernism in the nineteenth-century industrial centers of capitalism in Europe, particularly Paris, also saw the evolution of a new breed of artist who was an unclassed drifter and a spectator in the city. Baudelaire, Flaubert, Manet, and Toulouse-Lautrec all exemplify this type, which was cognate with the less artistic but equally observant and uncommitted man of the world.

O. Henry wrote a witty story about the American domestication of this type of sophisticated urban observer.[27] The story's narrator, curious to observe a man-about-town, makes a tour of all New York's nightspots without satisfying himself that he's located his quarry. Inattentive to traffic because of his absorption in this

28. An interesting response to Weegee's self-promoting tactics was expressed by Louis Stettner and James M. Zanutto in their article "Focus on Weegee," Popular Photography, April 1961. They compared Weegee to the celebrated French naive painter Le Douanier Rousseau, and then wrote of Weegee that "it must be recognized that his need to be talked about does not stem totally from personal vanity or insecurity. There is nothing basically wrong with a photographer's promoting his own fame, for if he is to continue working, fame or some sort of recognition is almost a necessary encouragement. It gives him not only the financial support he needs, but also assures his pictures an audience. Without it, talent usually does not grow. "

29. Weegee began contributing photographs to PM Daily soon after its founding in 1940. Its regular photographic staff included Margaret Bourke-White, Morris Engel, Irving Haberman, and Mary Morris, among others, and celebrated photographer Ralph Steiner was the photography editor. The paper's coverage of serious photography was unusually thorough and sophisticated. For instance, Paul Strand's book Photographs of Mexico received a brief review when it appeared (July 28, 1940, p. 40), as did Edward Weston's California and the West (December 8, 1940, p. 42).

The character of PM's typical features is nicely consonant with many of Weegee's subjects. For instance, the "Picture Gallery" section of the Sunday edition (PM's Weekly) for June 30, 1940, was devoted to "Seven Portraits of Sixth Ave.," a topic that might easily have suited Weegee's style, but which in fact was photographed by Bourke-White and Morris. On Monday, July 22, 1940, p. 12, a piece titled "New York Is a City of: People Who Work All Night" seems like an idea right out of Weegee's oeuvre; the five photographs were by Steven Derry and Ray Platnick. Another Sunday feature, "It's Been Hot—Some People Did Something About It" (July 28, 1940, pp. 14-17), includes views of people sleeping outdoors to beat the heat, playing in water in the streets, and going about their business as usual. Morris Gordon, Dan Israel, John DiBiase, William Wolford, and William Brunk are credited with the majority of the pictures, but the final image in the story is a Weegee self-portrait. Both in style and in subject, many of the PM staff photographers did work quite similar to Weegee's in many aspects.

Weegee himself became one of PM's subjects when he was profiled during a brief stay in Manhattan General Hospital for an operation. Obviously feeling rather well for a post-op patient, he was photographed in bed wearing his fedora, and managed to provide plenty of colorful copy about his philosophy of life. The piece is titled "Why Weegee Won't Marry a Brooklyn Girl" (April 21, 1946, p. 5).

30. Bruce Downes, "A Tribute," Weegee by Weegee, pp. 2-3. This theme was echoed even in Weegee's obituary in the New York Times, in which Harold Blumenfeld, the executive picture editor for UPI and formerly Weegee's boss at Acme Newspictures, was quoted as saying, "His pictures were not technically good, but they were great for subject material. He looked for subjects no one else ever found," New York Times, December 27, 1968, p. 33.

quest, he is knocked down in a street accident. When he returns to consciousness in a hospital ward, he's given a newspaper account of his own mishap, which closes by saying, "His injuries were not serious. He appeared to be a typical Man About Town." Though Weegee prowled through the city like this restless protagonist, he certainly wouldn't have been taken for a man-about-town under similar circumstances.

The *flaneur* drifts almost invisibly through the urban spectacles and throngs, observing, not being observed, consuming, not offering himself for consumption. Weegee, to say the least, lacked that genius for unobtrusiveness which is the hallmark of the true *flaneur*, who slips without identifying himself from one social arena to another, from the café to the club to strolling in the parks and boulevards of the city. Closer to a bum than a boulevardier, Weegee had a distinct presence on the scene: his class background was evident and his subjects engaged him vigorously. In his gregarious photograph "Crowd at Coney Island, Temperature 89 degrees" (pages 140-141), the many thousands of people crowded onto the beach seem to move as one to salute Weegee as he photographs them. His constant self-representation in his work, the relentless marketing of his work, his trademark name, and his larger-than-life persona have firmly established his character as an aspect of his work and as a presence in the history of photography.[28]

The good-natured, labor-oriented, frugal, humorous, optimistic, innocent (but far from naive) flavor of Weegee's photographs was not wholly original in his work and world view. PM Daily, the paper for which Weegee photographed for many years, shared much of this temperament and many of Weegee's preoccupations.[29] Perhaps PM's outlook was a bit more wholesome overall than Weegee's, but its concerns, tone, and style served as an essential model for him. The idea that Weegee's work was entirely unprecedented is as false as the notion that he was unskilled in photography. Weegee's frequently alleged artistic primitivism is belied by his sophistication as a visual thinker, a writer, and a well-read autodidact, yet this assessment of his work was even held by his friends and advocates. For instance, Bruce Downes, who wrote "A Tribute" for Weegee's autobiography, remarked: "Of any knowledge of art he was completely innocent. ... As the years went by he accumulated an impressive collection of pictures, the photographic quality of which was uniformly poor. But however bad they were technically, what was in them was true and alive."[30]

The myth of Weegee's lack of photographic skill is amply contradicted by the assurance, concision, and tremendously stylish composition of his pictures. Weegee's work was at first hard to appreciate because it didn't resemble other art photography of the day. It more nearly recalls the look of films noirs, which share with Weegee's work an emphasis on crime, drama, and dark urban passions. But there is a joyous and touching side to Weegee's images as well; he was a tough guy *and* a humanist.

Satirical humor as well as empathy diversifies the emotional range of Weegee's work beyond the raw images of corpses and tenement fires. He portrayed the "Naked City" during some of its most magical and dramatic years. These raucous, gritty, exuberant, and sometimes tender pictures convey the full panoply of life, work, play, sleep, and death in a great city. The persona Weegee created for himself was also not unlike those of Raymond Chandler's tough detectives, but he was too affable, sociable, voluble, boastful, and energetic to imitate very closely the more disaffected characters of such films and books. He was, after all, "Weegee the Famous," a self-promoting phenomenon of astonishing virtuosity.

Something has passed from the city in the years since Weegee photographed it. The problem, he suggested, was that by the late 1950s, "New York was in transition. My beloved slums were disappearing. The place where I had spent my happy childhood was now a housing project for the under-privileged. Everything in New York was becoming regimented. All television programs had to be approved by Paddy Chayevsky. All street fights and rumbles were under the supervision of the Police Athletic League."[31]

But perhaps the problem was simply that Weegee wasn't on the scene anymore. Today, the city is much the poorer, not for the loss of its slums, but rather for the loss of Weegee. Nonetheless, it has been permanently changed and enriched by Weegee's years of pounding the pavement, splitting the darkness with his flash, and plastering his images on newspaper pages and museum walls alike. Weegee called his camera "my modern Aladdin's lamp," and indeed it worked magic.[32] But the "lamp" he raised in the urban darkness bore some resemblance to that wielded by Diogenes as well. With it, he sought out honest men and rogues alike. Of the many visionaries and vision makers who have lived and worked in New York, it is Weegee whose imprint is deepest upon the city after fifty years. Perhaps this is because he came closest to recognizing the enduring character of this rebarbative town, as he captured the voice of the city in his photographs.

31. Weegee by Weegee, p. 135. On the other hand, Weegee was rather jaundiced in his view of the amenities offered by other towns. He summed up his contempt for Hollywood as follows: "The restaurants in Hollywood were simply awful. I judge a restaurant by their blintzes. I had eaten better blintzes—free—at the Salvation Army dinner on Christmas. Of course, since the natives are zombies, there were no rest-rooms in the Hollywood restaurants. (They drink formaldehyde instead of coffee, and have no sex organs.) In Hollywood, you can always recognize the out-of-towners . . . they carry their chamber-pots with them" (p. 102).

32. Dedication, Weegee by Weegee, np.

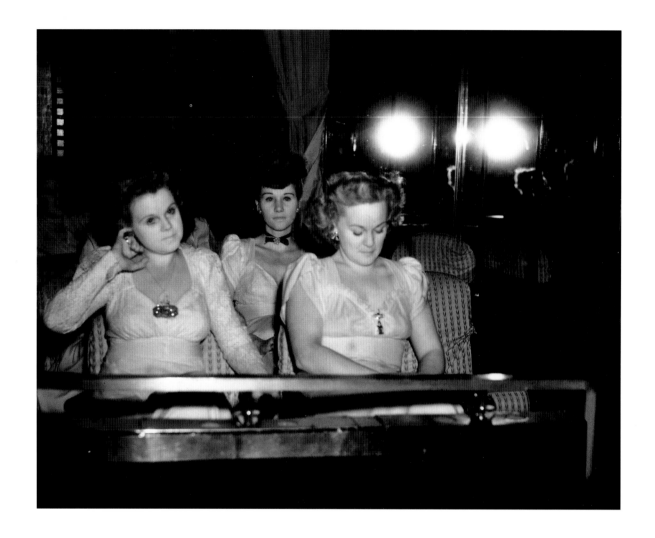

"Ten Cents a Dance," Roseland,
Times Square, c. 1943

"Dancing Tonite," New Gardens,
Times Square, c. 1944

# Dancing

## TO NITE

| Monday to Thursday | Music By | Friday, Sat. & Sunday |
| 20 Dances for $1.00 | Lionel Howard | 15 Dances for $1.00 |

*This woman is concerned about the D-Day Invasion, June 7, 1944*

*Woman looking at electric sign on the* New York Times *Building,* June 7, 1944

"The Faces of New York on Invasion Day," June 6, 1944

"A Trip To Mars," Times Square, c. 1943

*Viewing News Report of Yankee Game*, October 6, 1943

Macy's Parade – Clown and Crew, c. 1942

Macy's Santa, November 21, 1940

Woman Cab Driver and Macy's Clown, c. 1942

*Acrobat goes Head over Heels...*, c. 1943

"Radio City Music Hall Actor...," c. 1944

"The Opera Opened Last Night," Dec. 3, 1940

"The Socialites," c. 1941

*The Fashionable People*, [title first used for "The Critic" in *LIFE Magazine*], December 6, 1943

*In the Lobby at the Metropolitan Opera, Opening Night,*
November 22, 1943

*Metropolitan Opera's Women's Chorus Rehearsal,* November 26, 1944

*Metropolitan Opera's Men's Chorus Rehearsal,* November 26, 1944

*Champagne in ice bucket, c.1941*

*Opening Night, Metropolitan Opera, c. 1943* [Infrared Negative]

*Woman at Metropolitan Opera, c. 1943 [Infrared Negative]*

*Intermission, Metropolitan Opera, c. 1943 [Infrared Negative]*

"Louella Parsons at the Opera," c. 1945

*Opening Night at the 'Met'*, December 3, 1944
[Infrared Negative]

"Down With The Japs The Rats," October 18, 1942

"A Time of Great Optimism, and Lingering Doubt," May 7, 1945

*Subway Station serves as Blackout Shelter*, August 13, 1943

*V-J Day Victory Parade in Little Italy,* September 6, 1945

*Young East Siders Hang Hirohito in Effigy...*, October 11, 1942

"Time is Short," March 23, 1942

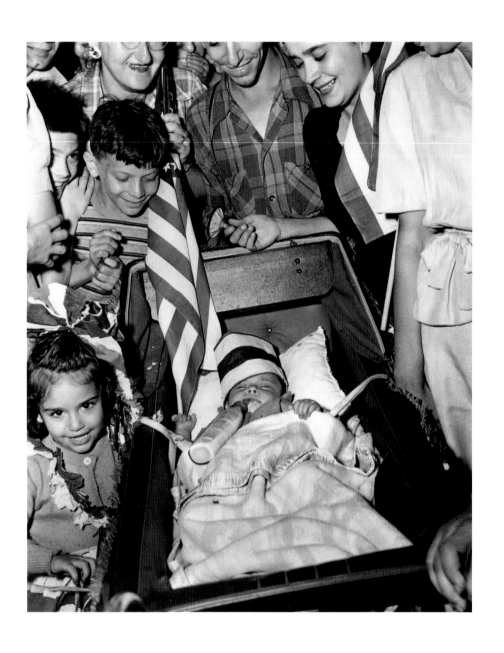

*Parades are so tiring...*, c. 1943

*Celebration at End of War,* c. 1945

"Der Fuehrer's Birthday," April 21, 1942

"There was Dancing in the Streets of New York," May, 1945

"TIMES SQUARE – early Tuesday morning," August, 1945

"Celebrating V-J Day at the Times Square Statute of Liberty,"
September, 1945

"There were Hugs for Everyone," c. 1945

*On top of the Empire State Building, c.1942*

*After midnight in Washington Square, Folk Dance, c.1955*

"Scene I – the Warm-up," c. 1948

"Scene II – the Kiss," c. 1948

"Scene III – the Clutch," c. 1948

"Alone in their dream," July 23, 1946

"Easter Sunday in Harlem," April 26, 1943

"Easter Sunday in Harlem," c. 1940

"Calypso," c. 1944

"She feels the BEAT...," c. 1944

"At the Jazz Concert," c. 1944

Boys Caught in Boarded-up Harlem Store,
August 16, 1943

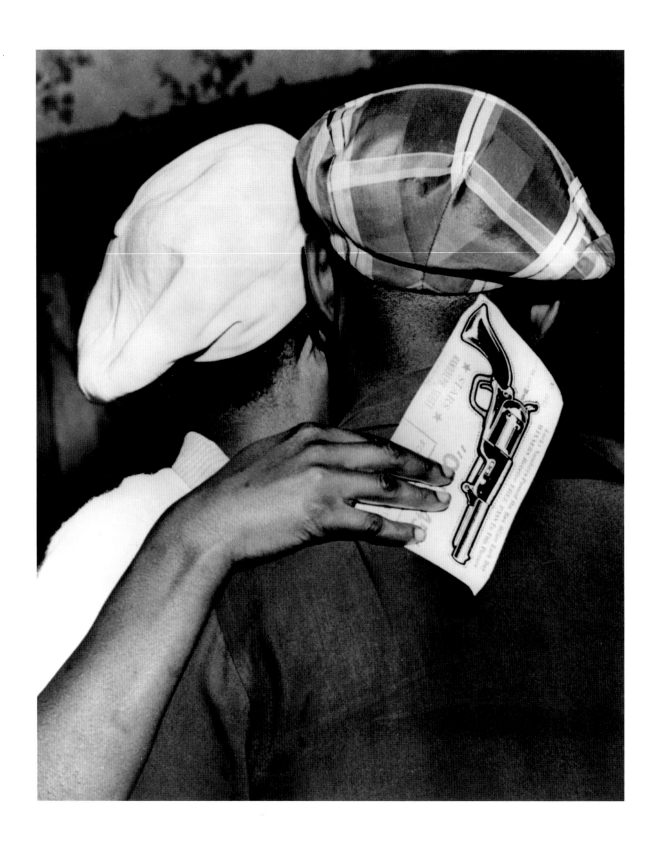

200          "The Lottery Ticket," c. 1950

"N. A. A. C. P.," c. 1943

"She's got the SPIRIT," c. 1943

"With a song in my heart," c. 1948

*Vera Middleton, Singer with Louie Armstrong, c. 1948*

"At a Jazz Concert," c. 1948

"Any Partner will do...," c. 1948

"This is a 'Frankie Fan'," October 12, 1944

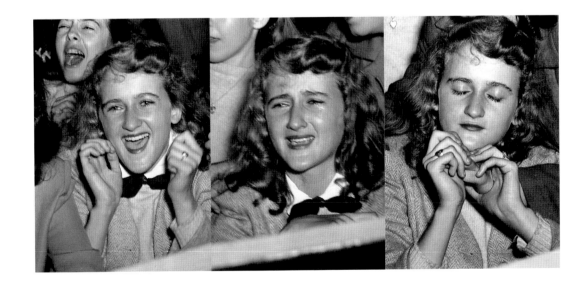

*Frank Sinatra, Paramount Theater,* October 12, 1944

"And a girl smiles to…Then she cries…The Swoon," November 5, 1944

"A phone booth is a handy place to make a date...," c. 1944

"Dressing Room at a New Orleans 'Burly-Que'," October 4, 1950

"Call Board," c. 1950

"Any bed will do...," c. 1950

"Sonata in G-Strings," c. 1950     211

*Audience listening to Jazz band playing "Bell Bottom Trousers," c. 1944*

*Women Listening to Bunk Johnson Concert*, Stuyvesant Casino, c. 1944

*Woman Calling out at Jazz concert*, Stuyvesant Casino, c. 1944

"Whistler's Mother," Arts Ball, Waldorf Astoria Hotel, New York, c. 1948

*Masquerade Ball*, Waldorf Astoria Hotel, c. 1943

*Audience in the Palace Theater*, c. 1950
[Infrared Negative]

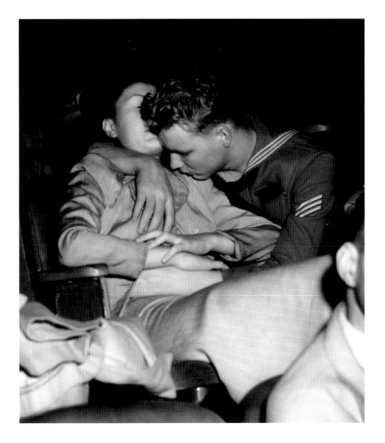

"Couple at the Palace Theater," c. 1943 [Infrared Negative]

"Lovers at the Palace Theater," c. 1945 [Infrared Negative]

*Sailor and girl at the movie*, c. 1943 [Infrared Negative]

*Children*, Palace Theater, c. 1943
[Infrared Negative]

*Children*, Palace Theater, c. 1943
[Infrared Negative]

*Girls watching movie*, Palace Theater, c. 1943
[Infrared Negative]

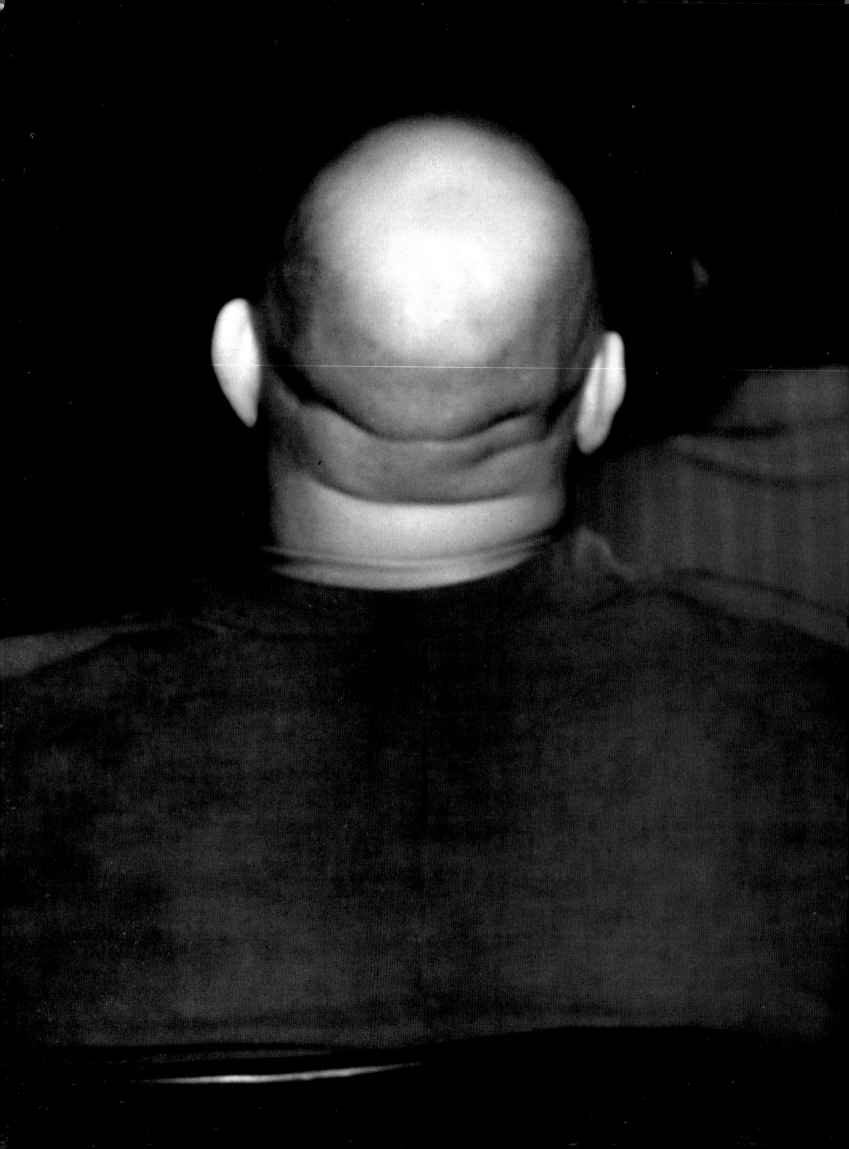

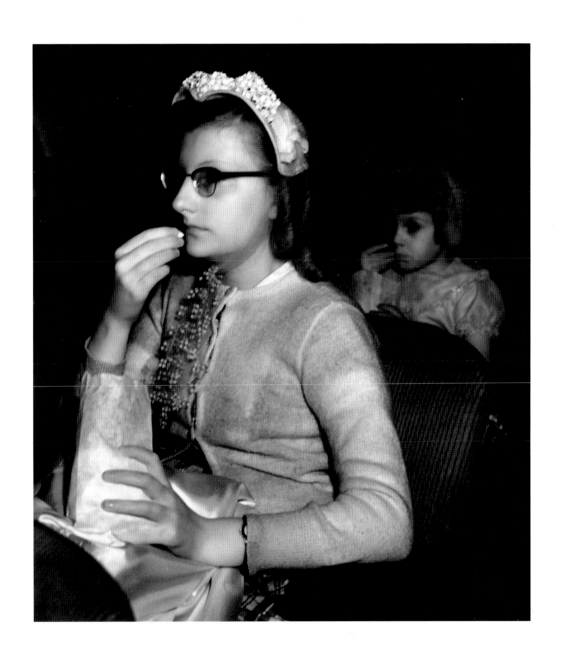

"The show's over," c. 1943
[Infrared Negative]

*Girl eating popcorn in the movies,* c. 1943
[Infrared Negative]

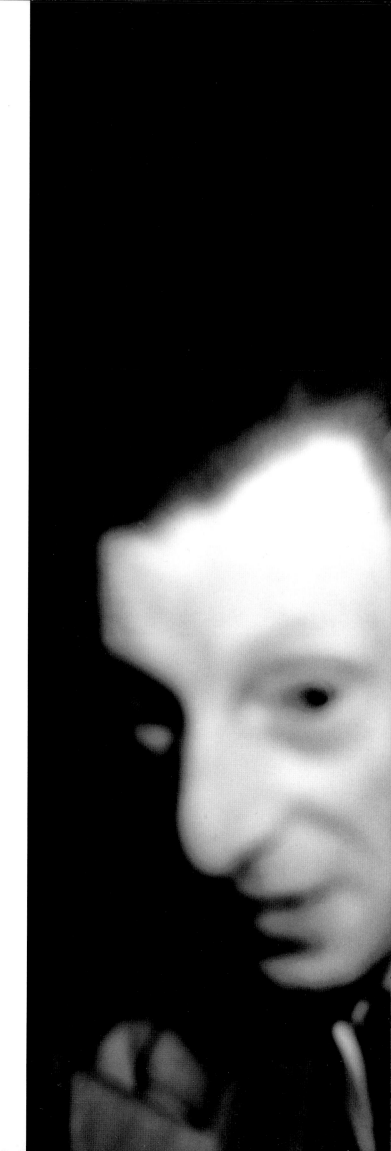

*Girls laughing at movie,* c. 1943
[Infrared Negative]

*Woman sleeping in movie theater*, c. 1943 [Infrared Negative]

*Sleeping at the movies*, c. 1943 [Infrared Negative]    *Overhead view of theater sleeper*, c. 1943 [Infrared Negative]

"Lovers at the Palace Theater I," c. 1945 [Infrared Negative]

"Lovers at the Palace Theater II," c. 1945 [Infrared Negative]

"Lovers at the Palace Theater III," c. 1945 [Infrared Negative]

"Lovers at the Palace Theater," c. 1945
[Infrared Negative]

"Tired Businessman at the Circus...," June 28, 1943

*Resourceful girl manages to watch man on the flying trapeze*
*and feed hot dog to escort at same time, April 18, 1943*

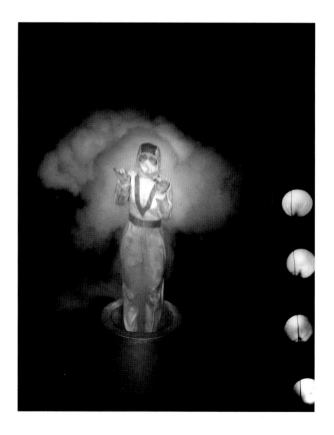

"Boom," June 28, 1943

"Here she comes," June 28, 1943

"She's almost out," June 28, 1943

"Off she goes," June 28, 1943

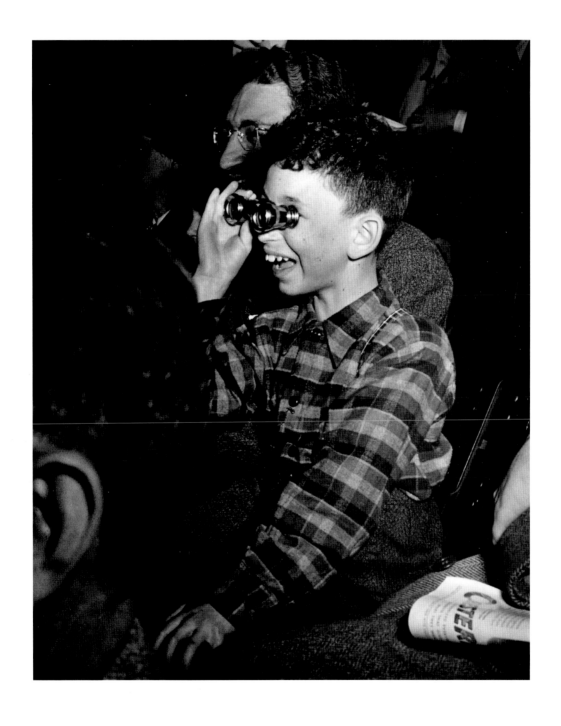

*Boy at circus, April 18, 1943*

"Circus Elephant at Madison Square Garden," c. 1942

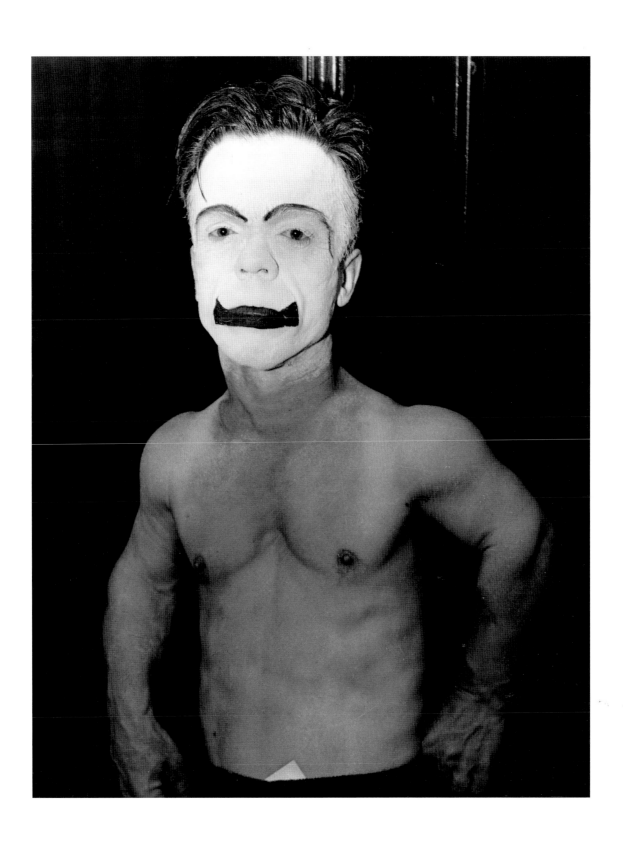

"Jimmy Armstrong, the Clown," c.1943

"Village Concert," c. 1951

"Blowing soap bubbles is fun, too…" Washington Square Park, c. 1944

"Girls at the Bar," c. 1946

"At San Ramo's," c. 1945

*Henry Fonda, Clark Gable and Bette Davis, Hollywood, c. 1949*

*Louie Armstrong, backstage at Basin Street,* New York, c. 1950

*Jimmy Durante surrounded by his young fans in Italian Restaurant, Little Italy, c. 1948*

242        "Stieglitz," May 7, 1944

"Lisette Model, at Nick's Jazz Joint," c. 1946

"Jerry Lewis and his friends," Hollywood, c. 1950          "Hopper's Topper," Hedda Hopper, Hollywood, c. 1948

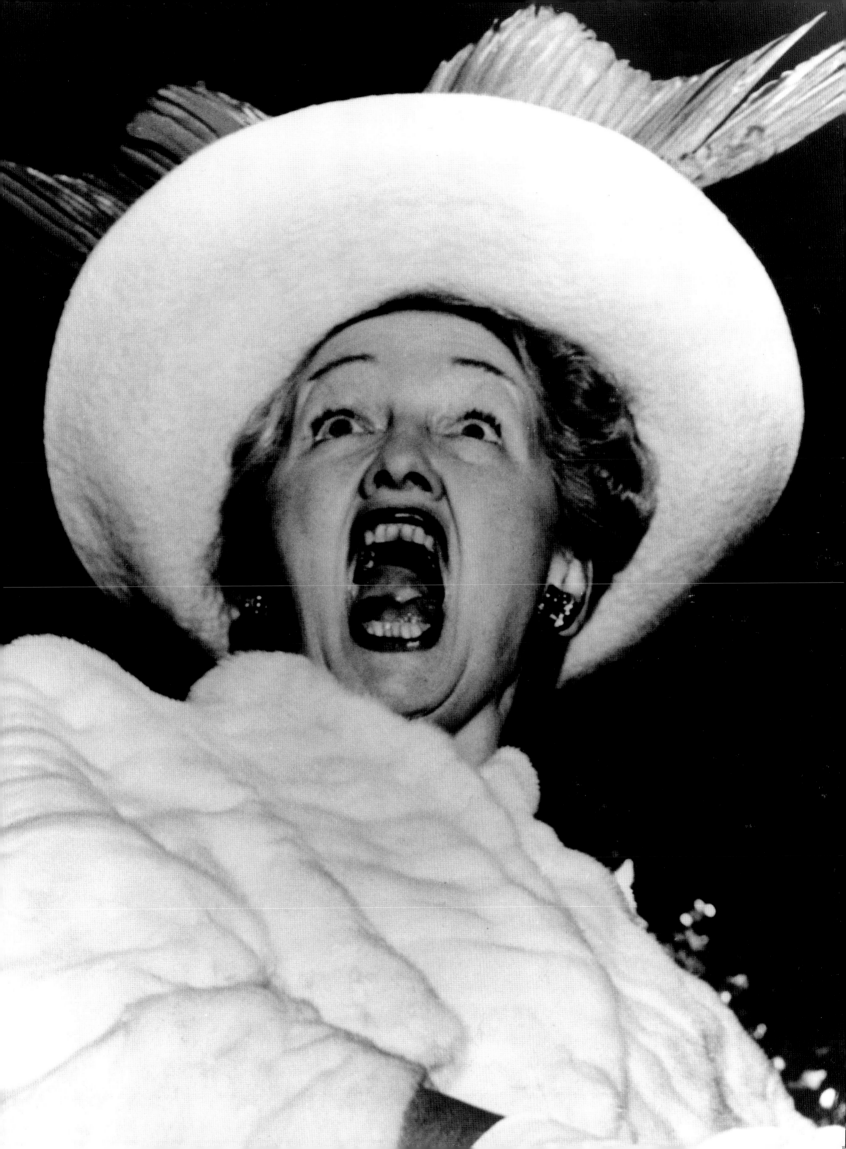

*Jayne Mansfield, Hollywood, c. 1951*

"DR. STRANGELOVE"
KUBRICK    CAMERAMAN G.TAYLOR
SCENE    TAKE
205    1
2 MARCH 1963    INT NIGHT.

"Peter Sellers, Stanley Kubrick, during filming of Dr. Strangelove." 1963

*The Rockettes* (kaleidoscope), c. 1958

*Zero Mostel – Samuel Joel*
(kaleidoscope), c. 1958

*Jerry Lewis* (kaleidoscope), c. 1956

Untitled (photomontage of Dora Pelletier, from 1941-an entertainer
at Sammy's-on-the-Bowery-inside a champagne bottle), c. 1959

Untitled (photomontage of "Lovers," July 1946
inside a perfume bottle), c. 1959

Untitled (photomontage of "Lovers" in Washington Square Park,
Greenwich Village, c. 1946 inside a half-gallon bottle), c. 1959

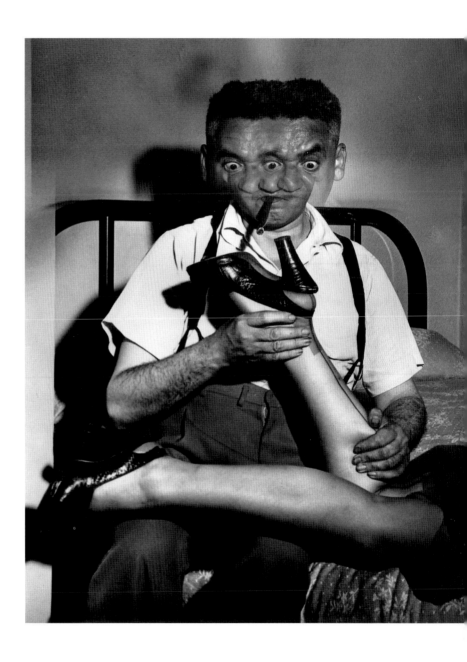

Marilyn Monroe (plastic lens), c. 1960

*Talent Scout in "Naked Hollywood"*
(self-portrait), c. 1950-52

Untitled (night club musician from c. 1946, plastic lens), c. 1960

*Tate Gallery, London* (plastic lens), c. 1960s

*London* (plastic lens), c. 1960

*Weegee and Model* (mirror effect/double image), c. 1953-56

*Nude* (mirror effect/double image), c. 1953-56
"Weegee's Women," *Showplace* [First Edition] (July 1956)

*Nude* (plastic lens and patterned glass), c. 1953-56
"Weegee's Women," *Showplace* [First Edition] (July 1956)

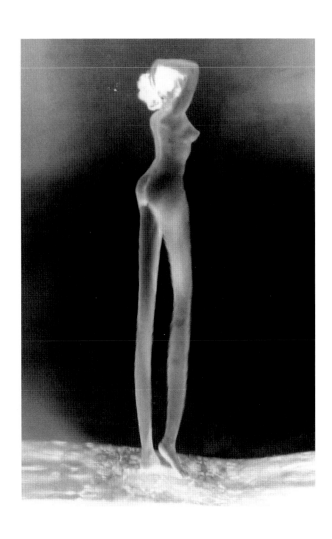

*Nude* (easel trick and plastic lens), c. 1953-56
"Weegee's Women," *Showplace* [First Edition] (July 1956)

251

## Weegee Chronology

**1899** Born Usher Fellig on June 12 in Lemberg (also known as Lvov), Austria (now Ukraine), to Rachel and Bernard Fellig. Weegee was the second of seven children. The first four, Elias (1897), Usher, Rachel, and Philip, were born in Lemberg. The youngest three siblings, Molly, Jack, and Yetta, were born in the United States.

**1906** Bernard Fellig leaves Europe for the United States.

**1910** Rest of family arrives in New York and settles on Manhattan's Lower East Side. Usher's name is changed to Arthur upon arrival. Bernard Fellig had studied to become a rabbi in Austria. However, in America, he earned a living as a pushcart vender, a common source of income for new immigrants on the Lower East Side. He and his wife also worked as janitors in a tenement building in exchange for rent. The elder Fellig always maintained a strong commitment to Judaism, maintaining the Sabbath even at the peril of the family's income. Later on in his life, Bernard Fellig completed his religious studies and became a rabbi.

**1913** Weegee (he will continue to be known as Arthur for the next two decades) makes the decision to leave school to help support his family. His first job was as a tintype photographer. After several months, Weegee started assisting a commercial photographer. After several years of grueling, tedious work, he quit to begin working as a street portrait photographer. Equipped with a pony, Weegee photographed Lower East Side children on weekends, making contact proofs during the week. This job was short-lived, however, because of the expense of caring for the pony.

**1917** At the demise of his pony photography career, Weegee decided to move out of his family home. He was eighteen and seeking freedom from his family's strict ways. For a time Weegee was homeless, and found shelter in missions and public parks, and Pennsylvania Railroad station. For several years, he held a variety of jobs including busboy, dishwasher, day laborer, candy mixer (including a stint as a "hole puncher" at the Life Saver factory), and biscuit maker. All the while, he regularly looked for work with a photography studio.

**1918** Weegee finds a job at Ducket & Adler photography studio on Grand Street in Lower Manhattan, where he does a variety of studio and darkroom tasks.

**1921** Applies for and receives a job as a helper in the darkrooms of the *New York Times*, and their photo syndicate Wide World Photos. This job was to last for two years.

**c.1924-27** Joins Acme Newspictures (later absorbed by United Press International) as darkroom technician and printer. While at Acme, filled in as news photographer.

**1934** Rents a one-room apartment at 5 Center Market Place, where he lives until 1947.

**1935** Leaves Acme to begin freelance career. Activities centered around Manhattan police headquarters. Photographs published by *Herald Tribune*, *World-Telegram*, *Daily News*, *Post*, *Journal-American*, *Sun*, and others. (This begins the period of Weegee's most significant work, produced in New York between 1935 and 1947.)

**1938** Obtains permission to install police radio in car. Around this time adopts name Weegee.

**1940** Given special position by the progressive evening newspaper *PM* to create photo-stories of his choice, or accept assignments from the newspaper's editors.

**1941** "Weegee: Murder Is My Business" exhibition opens at the Photo League, New York. Weegee begins to experiment with a handheld 16mm movie camera.

**1943** Five photographs acquired by The Museum of Modern Art, New York, and included in their exhibition "Action Photography."

**1945** Publication of *Naked City* (New York: Duell, Sloan & Pearce/ Essential Books), the first book of Weegee's photographs, and accompanying national publicity tour. Begins photographing for *Vogue*.

**1946** Publication of *Weegee's People* (New York: Duell, Sloan & Pearce/ Essential Books). Lectures at the New School for Social Research, New York. Weegee sells the rights to the title of his book, *Naked City*, to Mark Hellinger for a Hollywood feature film.

**1947** Marries Margaret Atwood, and late in this year leaves New York for Hollywood to serve as consultant on film version of *Naked City*. During the next several years, worked as technical consultant on films and played minor film roles. He also began to experiment with a variety of lenses and other devices to begin creating his "distortion" series.

**1948** Release of *The Naked City* by Universal Pictures, and Weegee appears for the first time as an extra in the film *Every Girl Should Be Married*. His own (and first) film, *Weegee's New York* (20 minutes, black and white, 16mm), is completed. He is represented in "50 Photographs by 50 Photographers," exhibition organized by Edward Steichen at The Museum of Modern Art, New York.

**1949** Weegee and Margaret Atwood are separated, and divorced a year later.

**c.1950** Produces film *Cocktail Party* (5 minutes, black and white, silent, 16mm).

**1952** Returns to New York after several years living and working in Hollywood. Begins a series of distorted portraits of celebrities and political figures, which he calls caricatures.

**1953** Publication of *Naked Hollywood* by Weegee and Mel Harris (New York: Pellegrini and Cudahy), the first book in which his distortions are published.

**1955** Distorted portraits are published in July issue of *Vogue*.

**1957** Diagnosed with diabetes, Weegee moves to West 47th Street, the home of Wilma Wilcox, who remains his companion until his death.

**1958** Consultant for Stanley Kubrick's film *Dr. Strangelove, or How I Learned to Stop Worrying and Love the Bomb*. Traveled extensively in Europe until 1968, working for the *Daily Mirror* and on a variety of photography, film, lecture, and book projects.

**1959** Lecture tour in USSR in conjunction with several exhibitions held here.

Publication of *Weegee's Creative Camera* (Garden City, NJ: Hanover House).

**1960** Exhibition: "Weegee: Caricatures of the Great," at Photokina, Cologne, West Germany.

**1961** Publication of autobiography, *Weegee by Weegee* (New York: Ziff-Davis).

**1962** Exhibition at Photokina, Cologne, West Germany.

**1964** Publication of *Weegee's Creative Photography* (London: Ward, Lock, and Co.).

**c.1965** Makes film *The Idiot Box* (5 minutes, black and white, sound, 16mm).

**1968** Weegee dies in New York on December 26, age 69.

# Bibliography

## Books by Weegee

*Naked City.* New York: Duell, Sloan, & Pearce/Essential Books, 1945.

*Naked City,* 2nd Rev. Ed. New York: DaCapo Press, 1973.

*Weegee's People.* New York: Duell, Sloan, & Pearce/Essential Books, 1946.

*Weegee's People.* 2nd Rev. Ed. New York: DaCapo Press, 1975.

*Naked Hollywood.* Weegee and Mel Harris. New York: Pellegrini and Cudahy, 1953.

*Naked Hollywood.* 2nd Rev. Ed. Weegee and Mel Harris. New York: DaCapo Press, 1975.

*Weegee's Secrets of Shooting with Photo Flash as Told to Mel Harris.* New York: Hartis Publishers, 1953.

*Weegee's Creative Camera.* Weegee and Ron Ald. Garden City, NJ: Hanover House, 1959.

*Weegee's Creative Photography.* London: Ward, Lock, and Co., 1964.

*Weegee by Weegee: An Autobiography.* New York: Ziff-Davis Publishing Company, 1961.

*The Village.* New York: DaCapo Press, Inc., 1989. (Published posthumously.)

## Books About Weegee

COPLANS, John. *Weegee's New York: Photographs 1935-1960.* Munich, GmbH: Schirmer Art Books, Schirmer/Mosel Verlag, 1982.

COPLANS, John. *Weegee: Violenti e Violentati.* Milan: G. Mazzotta, 1979.

LAUDE, Andre. *Weegee.* Paris: Centre National de la Photographie, 1985.

LIPTON, Norman C. *So You Want to Be a Free-Lance!* Jackson Heights, NY: Fawcett Publications, 1941.

LIPTON, Norman C. *"Weegee" Top Free-Lance Tells How He Does It!,* Photography Handbook #10. Jackson Heights, NY: Fawcett Publications, 1942.

MARSHALL, Joseph. *Weegee the Famous and the New York Milieu.* Unpublished Ph.D. dissertation, the University of New Mexico, 1993.

NOTHHELFER, Gabriele. *Bildinterprationen zu Fotografien von Weegee.* Berlin, Germany: A. Nagel, 1978.

PORTER, Allan, intro. *Weegee 1899 - 1968. Photothema, 10.* Zurich: U. Bar Verlag, 1991.

STETTNER, Louis, ed. *History of the Nude in American Photography.* Greenwich, CT: Whitestone Book/Fawcett-Haynes Printing Corporation, 1966 (chapter 13, pp. 106-109).

STETTNER, Louis, ed. *Weegee.* New York: Alfred A. Knopf, 1977.

TALMEY, Allene and Martin Israel. *Weegee.* Aperture History of Art Series, 8. New York: Aperture, Inc., 1978.

## Articles About Weegee

ALETTI, Vince. "Art: Louis Faurer, Leon Levinson, Lisette Model, Weegee," *Village Voice*, vol. 40, no. 23 (June 6, 1995), p. SS10A.

ARNESON, Rosemary. "Video Review – The Real Weegee," *Library Journal,* vol. 114, no. 19 (November 15, 1989), p. 116.

BADGER, Gerry. "Viewed: Weegee 'The Famous' at Stills Gallery, Edinburgh," *British Journal of Photography,* vol. 126, no. 14 (April 6, 1979), pp. 324-327.

BARRY, Les. "Weegee Covers the Circus," *Popular Photography,* vol. 42, no. 4 (April 1958), pp. 126-127.

BERG, Gretchen. "Naked Weegee," *Photograph,* vol. 1, no. 1 (1976), pp. 1-4, 24, 26.

BLUMENFELD, Harold. "Weegee the Photographer Dies, Chronicled Life of Naked City," *New York Times* (December 27, 1968), p. 33.

BLUMENFELD, Harold. "Weegee: Alias Arthur Fellig," *Photographic Business and Product News* (February 1969), pp. 22-24, 42-43.

CALLAHAN, Sean. "Photography: American Photography's Greatest Primitive Has Left Us a Message," *Village Voice* (November 3, 1975), pp. 132-133.

CARLUCCIO, Luigi. "*Venezia '79: La Fotographia* Weegee," *Panorama* (August 27, 1979), p. 13.

COLEMAN, A. D. "Weegee as Printmaker: An Anomaly in the Marketplace," *Journal of American Photography,* vol. 3, no. 1 (March 1985), pp. 4-6.

COPLANS, John. "Photography: Weegee the Famous," *Art in America* (September-October 1977), pp. 37-41.

COREY, David. "Weegee's Unstaged Coney Island Dramas," *American Art* (Winter/Spring 1991), pp. 16-21.

DENBY, David. "Weegee Bored: *The Public Eye* Directed by Howard Franklin," *New York Magazine,* vol. 25, no. 43 (November 2, 1992), pp. 73-74.

EDWARDS, Owen. "Streets Seen: Why Photographers Will Take Manhattan," *American Photographer,* vol. 16 (May 1986), pp. 32, 34.

EDWARDS, Owen. "What Becomes a Photo Most?" *American Photographer,* vol. 20 (June 1988), pp. 54-58.

EVANS-CLARK, Phillip. "Weegee," *Arts Magazine,* vol. 63, no. 5 (June 1989), p. 78.

FONDILLER, Harvey V. "Critics at Large: Weegee's Living Screen," *Popular Photography,* vol. 59, no. 3 (September 1966), p. 44.

FONDILLER, Harvey V. "Gravure Portfolio: Weegee's New York," *Popular Photography,* vol. 82, no. 6 (June 1978), pp. 120-129.

FONDILLER, Harvey V., Norman Rothchild and David Vestal. "Weegee: A Lens on Life, 1899-1968," *Popular Photography,* vol. 64, no. 4 (April 1969), pp. 92-95, 100.

FULLER, Graham. "Don't Blink Say Weegee," *Interview,* vol. 22 (October 1992), pp. 134-137.

GOLDMAN, Judith. "Weegee the Famous," *Quest/77,* vol. 1, no. 4 (September/October 1977), pp. 69-74.

GREENBERG, Clement. "Four Photographers: Eugene-August Atget, Edward Steichen, Andreas Feininger and Henri Cartier-Bresson," *New York Review of Books* (January 23, 1964), pp. 8-9. Reprinted in *History of Photography,* Summer 1991, pp. 131-132.

HOBERMAN, J. "American Abstract Sensationalism," *Artforum* (February 1981), pp. 42-49.

LEE, David. "Weegee in England," *British Journal of Photography,* vol. 128, no. 36 (September 4, 1981), pp. 902-903, 914.

LIFSON, Ben. "Photography: Weegee: Acquainted with the Night," *Village Voice,* vol. 22, no. 43 (October 24, 1977), p. 101.

LOPATIN, Judy. "Retrospective on Weegee," *CEPA Quarterly,* vol. 3, no. 1 (Fall 1987), pp. 11-14.

MALONEY, Russell. "Portraits of a City," *New York Times Book Review* (July 22, 1945), p. 5.

MARTIN, Murray. "Flash Suit, Flash Myth: An Interview with Weegee's Widow, Wilma Wilcox," *Creative Camera,* no. 218 (February 1983), pp. 834-837.

MEETZE, Florence. "How 'Pop' Photo Crashes an Opening," *Popular Photography,* vol. 1, no. 8 (December 1937), pp. 36-38, 80-81.

MESSADIE, Gerard. "Weegee le Truculent," *Photo Cine Revue* (May 1980), pp. 258-261.

MUCHNIC, Suzanne. "Art Review: Weegee's Camera Sees Everything," *Los Angeles Times* (December 9, 1986), pp. 1, 6.

ORVELL, Miles. "Weegee's Voyeurism and the Mastery of Urban Disorder," *American Art*, vol. 6, no. 1 (Winter 1992), pp. 18-41.

PARSONS, Marc J. "Weegee's Wedding," *Minicam Photography* (June 1947), pp. 40-44, 105.

QUINDLEN, Anna. "He Was There," *New York Times Magazine* (September 11, 1977), pp. 40-43.

REILLY, Rosa. "Freelance Cameraman," *Popular Photography*, vol. 1, no. 8 (December, 1937), pp. 21-23, 76-79.

REYNOLDS, Charles. "Credit Photo by Weegee the Famous: 1899-1969," *Infinity* (December 1968), p. 19.

ROSENBLUM, Walter. "Weegee's New York Photographs 1935-1960," *Exposure* (Summer 1985), pp. 38-41.

SCULLY, Julia. "Seeing Pictures: Weegee the Famous, Turned News Photos into Powerful Social Documents. What Made Weegee Run?" *Modern Photography,* vol. 41, no. 12 (December 1977), pp. 8, 10, 24, 28.

STEINER, Ralph. "Weegee Lives for His Work and Thinks Before Shooting," *PM Weekly* (March 9, 1941), pp. 48-51.

STETTNER, Louis. "Uncouth Genius," (London) *Photography*, vol. 15, no. 12 (December 1960), pp. 34- 41.

STETTNER, Louis, and James M. Zanutto. "Focus on Weegee," *Popular Photography*, vol. 48, no. 4 (April 1961), pp. 40-41, 101-102.

STETTNER, Louis. "Speaking Out: Weegee, Naked City's Forgotten Man," *Camera 35*, vol. 15, no. 7 (September 1971), pp. 14-15.

STETTNER, Louis. "Cezanne's Apples and the Photo League," *Aperture*, no. 124 (Summer 1991), pp. 14-35.

STEVENS, Mark. "The Bad and the Beautiful," *Newsweek*, vol. 90, no. 13 (September 16, 1977), pp. 72-73.

STRAND, Paul. "Weegee Gives Journalism a Shot for Creative Photography," *PM Daily* (July 22, 1945), p. 13.

STUART, Anne. "Photographer of the City," *Newsday* (July 4, 1985), Sec. II, pp. 2-3.

SUSSMAN, Aaron. "The Little Man Who's Always There," *Saturday Review of Literature* (July 28, 1945), p. 17.

THORNTON, Gene. "Photography View: The Satirical, Sentimental Weegee," *New York Times* (September 18, 1977), Sec. II, p. 29.

TILESTON, Nathaniel. "Weegee the Famous: International Center of Photography," *SoHo Weekly News* (September 22, 1977), p. 23.

TOBIAS, Tobi. "Weegee Is Her Muse," *New York* (September 12, 1994), pp. 90-91.

TYTELL, Mellyn and John Tytell. "Encounters: The Houdini of Photography," *Camera Arts,* vol. 1, no. 3 (May/June 1981), pp. 34-35, 105.

WEEGEE. "Travel: A New York Police Reporter's Impression of Washington," *PM Weekly* (March 2, 1941), p. 50.

WEEGEE. "House of 1,000 Girls," *Stag* (January 1951), pp. 16-17, 70-71.

WEEGEE. "Foto Finish," *New York Item* (June 22, 1961), p. 6-7.

WESTERBECK, Colin L., Jr. "Night Light: Brassaï and Weegee," *Artforum*, vol. 15, no. 4 (December 1976), pp. 34-45.

WILSON, Earl. "Weegee: New York's Free-est Freelance Cameraman," *Saturday Evening Post*, vol. 215, no. 47 (May 22, 1943), pp. 37, 39.

WOLBARST, John. "Weegee Goes to 35 mm," *Modern Photography,* vol. 18, no. 10 (October 1954), pp. 100-101.

YOUNG, Mort. "Weegee's Lens Show Is Kissed Off," *World Journal-Tribune* (April 13, 1967), p. 27.

ZITO, Tom. "Weegee's New York," *Washington Post* (November 2, 1977), pp. B1, B2.


## Unsigned Articles About Weegee

"Speaking of Pictures: A Free Lance Photographs the News," *LIFE* (April 12, 1937), pp. 8, 9, 11.

"The Press: Weegee," *LIFE* (July 23, 1945), pp. 70-71.

"Modest and Assuming," *Newsweek,* vol. 26, no. 4 (July 23, 1945), pp. 70-71.

"Speaking of Pictures: Weegee Shows How to Photograph a Corpse," *LIFE* (August 12, 1945), pp. 8-9, 11.

"In New York – Victory V's of Blazing Sawdust: VJ Day, New York – Photographed Especially for Vogue by Weegee," *Vogue,* vol. 106, no. 4 (September 1, 1945), pp. 116-117.

"Weegee's People," *Minicam Photography*, vol. 10, no. 6 (March 1947), pp. 60-63.

"2 Billion Clicks: A Half Century of U.S. Photography," *Time* (November 2, 1953), pp. 58-74.

"Weegee," *Creative Camera*, no. 61 (July 1969), pp. 252-259.


## Articles About Weegee's "Distortions"

BUCHWALD, Art. "Weegee's Looking For New Angles." *New York Herald Tribune* (January 24, 1960), sec. 4, p. 3.

FONDILLER, Harvey V. "Weegee Unveils His Plastic Lens." *Popular Photography,* vol. 61 (August 1967), p. 115.

GLASSMAN, Leo. "World's Top Photog to Write Column for New York Item." *New York Item,* vol. 3, no. 6 (June 1, 1961), pp. 1, 3.

GLASSMAN, Leo. "Big Mouth In Trouble." *New York Item,* vol. 3, no. 9 (June 22, 1961), p. 3.

JOHNSON, Hope. "A Cameraman Crashes the Pop Art Act." *New York World-Telegram* (April 11, 1966), p. 21.

LICHELLO, Bob. "The Famous Weegee Wants a Woman from Mars Because. . . Ladies You're Not Human!" *National Enquirer* (August 4, 1957), pp. 5, 12.

MANCEAUX, Michele. "La Semaine." *L'Express* (January 21, 1960), p. 34.

MOLEN, F. v. d. "Weegee Trekt de Wereld Het Masker Af," *Elseviers Weekblad* (September 23, 1961), p. 1.

WEEGEE. "Camera Caricatures." *New York Item* (June 15, 1961), p. 21.

WEEGEE. "Camera Caricatures." *New York Express* (October 5, 1964), p. 10.

WEEGEE. "Foto Finish." *New York Item*, vol. 3, no. 8 (June 15, 1961), p. 7.

WEEGEE. "Here's Fun from My Bag of Camera Tricks." *Popular Mechanics*, no. 105 (April 1956), pp. 126-131.

WEEGEE. "Photo Designs." *Photography Handbook*, no. 374 (1958), pp. 12-19.

WEEGEE. "Presenting: The Candidates as Seen Through the Three Eyes of Weegee: One of America's Outstanding Photographers." *See* (October 1968), p. 26-27, 31.

WEEGEE. "Weegee's Women." *First Edition Showplace* (July 1956), pp. 4-11, 40-42.

WHITCOMB, Noel. "The World's Craziest Cameraman Takes a Look at Mr. MacMillian: They're Weegee's!" [New York] *Daily Mirror* (March 21, 1960), pp. 13.

## Unsigned Articles About Weegee's Distortions

"Speaking of Pictures: Artful Tricks with a Mirror Create a Gallery of Satirical Partial Portraits." *LIFE*, vol. 37, no. 22 (November 29, 1954), pp. 10-11.

"Weegee's Kaleidoscope." *Popular Photography*, vol. 36, no. 2 (February 1955), pp. 52-53.

"Stretch Caricatures." *Vogue*, 126 (July 1955), pp. 74-77.

"What's Happening to Venus?" *Parade* (November 6, 1955), p. 4.

"How Your TV Heroes Look to a Weegee Magic Camera." *Look*, 20 (May 1, 1956), pp. 62-65.

"West vs. East with a Magic Camera." *Look*, vol. 20, no. 16 (August 7, 1956), pp. 42-43.

"Weegee's Photo Tricks." *Photography Handbook*, no. 327 (1956), pp. 23-25.

"How Weegee Made His Caricatures of Four Famous Photographers." *Popular Photography* (September 1956), pp. 44, 77, 80.

"Weegee's Spoofs the New Spring Hats." *Look*, vol. 21 (April 16, 1957), pp. 88-91.

"Weegee Puts Mirrors on His Bolex." *Bolex Reporter* (Spring 1958), pp. 12-13, 31.

"Weegee macht camera ..." *Bild am Sonntag* (December 13, 1959), p. 14.

"Reflective Photography." *The* [London] *Times* (October 11, 1960), p. 2.

"Weegee, de wonder." [Holland] *Actueel! Panorama* (December 17, 1960), p. 51.

"Weegee Views Summit: Big Two Prey of Famed Photog's Satire." *New York Item*, vol. 3, no. 8 (June 15, 1961), p. 1.

" 'Fantasmagoria Ball' – The Party of the Year: Costume Fete a Big Success." *New York Item*, vol. 3, no. 8 (June 15, 1961), p. 6.

"Weegee's New York Is Year-Round Madness." *New York Item*, vol. 12 (July 13, 1961), p. 6.

"Il Fotografo Cattivo." *Epoca* (December 2, 1962), pp. 29-30.

"What Did Weegee Do?" *Popular Photography*, vol. 52, no. 2 (February 1963), pp. 56-57.

"They Tried to Match Weegee," *Popular Photography*, vol. 53, no. 6 (July 1963), pp. 68-69.

"Art or Gimmick?" *South Wales Echo* (November 11, 1963), p 6.

"It's Just Crazy!" [Edinburgh, UK] *Evening News and Dispatch* (November 21, 1963), p. 4.

"Weegee la combine." (Paris) *Photo*, no. 133 (October 1978), pp. 44-51, 102.

## Filmography

### Films with Weegee as Advisor, Technical Staff, and/or Actor

**The Naked City**
Mark Hellinger *Prod. Dist.* Universal International Pictures. 1948. B/W. 96 min.
*Dir.* - Jules Dassin.
*Consultant, still photographer* - Weegee.
Weegee - *Extra* - Street photographer.

**Every Girl Should Be Married**
*Dist.* RKO Pictures. 1948, B/W. 86 min.
Weegee - *Extra* - Street photographer.

**The Set Up**
*Dist.* RKO Studio. 1949. B/W. 85 min.
*Technical advisor* - Weegee.
Weegee - *Bit part* - Timekeeper.

**The Yellow Cab Man**
*Dist.* Metro Goldwyn Mayer Pictures. 1950. B/W. 85 min.
*Special effects* - Weegee.
Weegee - *Bit role* - Cab driver.

**Journey into Light**
Joseph Bernhard *Prod. Dist.* 20th Century Fox. 1951. B/W, 87 min.
*Prod.* - Joseph Bernhard.
*Special photography* - Weegee.
Weegee - *Extra* - Skid Row bum.

**Windjammer**
Cinemiracle *Prod. Dist.* National Theatres. 1958. Eastman color. 150 min.
*Prod.* - Louis de Rochemont.
*Specialty photography* - Weegee.
Weegee - *Bit part* - New York street cameraman.

**Shangri-La**
Shangri-La *Prod. Dist.* Joseph Brenner Associates. 1961. Eastman color. 35mm. 64 min.
*Prod.* - Dick Randall.
*Special photography* - Weegee.

**The Magic Fountain**
Allan David *Prod. Dist.* Classic World Films. Davis Film Distributors. 1961. Eastman color. 35 mm (Ultrascope). 82 min.
*Prod. - Dir.* Allan David.
*Special effects* - Weegee.
Weegee - *Extra* - Villager.

**Dr. Strangelove, or How I Learned to Stop Worrying and Love the Bomb**
Hawks *Prod. Dist.* Columbia Pictures. 1963. B/W. 93 min.
*Prod. - Dir.* - Stanley Kubrick.
*Special effects consultant* - Weegee.

## Films by Weegee

*Weegee's New York,* 1948, 16 mm, B/W and color, 20 min. (original title, *Manhattan Moods*).

*Cocktail Party,* c.1950, 16 mm, B/W, 5 min.

*Hollywood - Land of the Zombie,* c.1950, 16 mm, B/W.

*San Francisco,* c.1950 (no known copy in existence).

*BOAC and Other Assorted Scenes,* 1955-1959, 16 mm, B/W and color, 5 min.

*Animation - Mona Lisa,* 1955-1959, 16 mm, B/W and color, 5 min.

*The Idiot Box,* c.1965, 16 mm, B/W, 5 min.

*Fun City,* 1967, 16 mm, color and B/W, undetermined length.

## Films About Weegee

*Weegee in Hollywood,* by Erven Jourdan and Esther McCoy, 1950, 16 mm, B/W, 10 min.

*The Naked Eye,* by Louis Clyde Stoumen, Camera Eyes Pictures, Inc., 1956, 16 mm, B/W and color, 71 min.

*Berumte Weegee, Der,* Westdeutscher Rundfunk Prod., 1987, color, 55 min, Knut Fischer, Prod.

## Videos About Weegee

*The Real Weegee,* Sherman Price Productions, 1987, color and B/W, video, 58 min.

*Weegee's Widow,* An interview with Wilma Wilcox, BBC Prod., Distributor; Arena Film, 1992, B/W, 27 min.

## Exhibitions

### Individual Exhibitions

1941 "Weegee: Murder Is My Business," Photo League, New York (August).

"Weegee: Murder Is My Business II," Photo League, New York (September).

1959 "Weegee," Moscow (traveled throughout USSR, as part of lecture tour).

1960 "Weegee: Caricatures of the Great," Photokina, Cologne, West Germany.

1962 "Weegee," Photokina, Cologne, West Germany.

1975 "Weegee," Center for Creative Photography, Tucson, Arizona.

1976 "Weegee," Marcuse Pfeiffer Gallery, New York.

1977 "Weegee, the Famous," International Center of Photography, New York.

1978 "Weegee," Galerie Zabriskie, Paris.

1979 "Weegee, 'The famous'," Stills Gallery, Edinburg, Scotland.

1980 "Weegee," Side Gallery, New Castle-upon-Tyne, England.

"Weegee," Daniel Wolf Gallery, New York.

"Weegee," The Photographer's Gallery, London.

1981 "Weegee the Famous," Port Washington Public Library, Port Washington, New York.

1984 "Weegee and The Human Comedy," San Francisco Museum of Modern Art.

"Weegee," Boston University Art Gallery, Massachusetts.

1985 "Two's Company," Light Gallery, New York.

1986 "Weegee," Allentown Art Museum, Pennsylvania.

"Weegee," Lawrence Miller Gallery, New York.

1992 "Weegee," Pace-MacGill Gallery, New York.

"Portrait of a City," Janet Borden Gallery, New York.

1995 "Weegee: The Photography of Arthur Fellig," David Winton Bell Gallery, Brown University, Rhode Island.

1996 "Weegee," Artspace Shiseido Gallery, Tokyo, Japan.

### Group Exhibitions

1943 "Action Photography," The Museum of Modern Art, New York.

1944 "Art in Progress," The Museum of Modern Art, New York.

1948 "50 Photographs by 50 Photographers," organized by Edward Steichen, The Museum of Modern Art, New York.

1962 "Photo Group Exhibition," Ligoa Duncan Art Centre, Paris.

1967 "Photography in the Twentieth Century," National Gallery of Canada, Ottawa (toured Canada and the United States, 1967-1973).

1970 "Into the 70's, 16 Artist Photographers," Akron Art Institute, Ohio.

1974 "News Photography," The Museum of Modern Art, New York.

"Photography in America," Whitney Museum of American Art, New York.

1977 "Documenta 6," Kassel, Germany.

1978 "Tusen och En Bild/ 1001 Pictures," Moderna Museet, Stockholm, Sweden.

1979 "Photographie als Kunst 1879 - 1979/ Kunst als Photographie 1949-1970." Tiroler Landesmuseum Fredinandeum, Innsbruck, Austria. (Traveled to Neue Galerie der Stadt Linz, Wolfgang - Gurlitt - Museum, Linz, Austria; Neue Galerie am Landesmuseum Joanneum, Graz, Austria and Museum des 20. Jahrhunderts, Vienna, Austria.)

"America Fotografsfie 1920-1940," Kunsthaus, Zurich, Switzerland.

1980 "Southern California Photography 1900-1965," Los Angeles County Museum of Art, California.

"50 Original Photographs, 1930's - 1960's, plus Three Designers," Fine Art Gallery, Montana State University, Bozeman, Montana.

1982 "Floods of Light," The Photographer's Gallery, London (toured Britain).

1983 "Weegee/Arbus/ Model/ Thompson," Haverford College, Pennsylvania.

1984 "Sammlung Gruber," Museum Ludwig, Cologne, West Germany.

1985 "American Images: Photographers 1945-1980," Barbican Art Gallery, London, England (toured Britain).

1986 "A Photographic Mix," Vision Gallery, San Francisco, California.

"Picture Taking," Mary and Leigh Block Gallery, Northwestern University, Chicago.

1989 "On the Art of Fixing a Shadow: One Hundred and Fifty Years of Photography," National Gallery of Art, Washington, D.C. (Traveled to Art Institute of Chicago and Los Angeles County Museum of Art.)

1990 "Arbus and Weegee: Photographs," Robert Klein Gallery, Boston.

1996 "An American Century of Photography: From Dry-Plate to Digital," Hallmark Photographic Collection. Museum of Photographic Arts, San Diego, California.

"The Big City," Boston Museum of Fine Arts, Massachusetts.

"New York, New York: The City of Ambition," Whitney Museum of American Art, New York.

# Extended Captions

8. Photographer unknown. *Portrait of Weegee (Arthur Fellig)*, c. 1956
Inscribed on image: "To all my Subjects, Weegee."

13. Photographer unknown. *Weegee's parents – Rachel and Bernard Fellig*, c. 1920s

16. Photographer unknown. *Weegee playing poker at Acme Newspictures*, c. 1927

17. Photographer unknown. *Weegee and fellow press photographers in front of Police Headquarters*, c. 1934

18. Photographer unknown. *Weegee at Police Headquarters with Teletype Machine*, c. 1934-36

20. Photographer unknown. *Weegee's Police Department Auto Radio Receiving Set Permit*, c. 1940

21. Photographer unknown. *Weegee at his typewriter in the trunk of his 1938 'Chevy'*, c. 1943

24. *Coney Island at noon Saturday, July 5th, 1942*
"The crowd came later according to Weegee who wanted a photo that showed some beach and not too many people. The masked man said he was a laundry man, but would only be photographed incognito. The mask is a gag of his; he calls himself the Spider, and likes to frighten people. Weegee didn't get the names and addresses of the others in the photo, either." PM Story and Photo by Weegee.

25. *Lovers After Dark, Coney Island*, c. 1943. *Naked City*.

27. *"The Critic,"* November 22, 1943, first published in *LIFE*, December 6, 1943

28. *Installation view of Weegee's exhibition in "Art in Progress,"* Museum of Modern Art, New York, 1944

31. "Weegee, as Clown, Covers Circus From the Inside," July 9, 1943
"Waiting backstage and my mind on my acting, just before I went on. The cutie limbering up is one of the Novelle sisters...." PM Photo by Weegee.

34. Photographer unknown. *Weegee with Advertisement for publication of Secrets of Flash Photography*, c. 1953

## LOWER EAST SIDE (pp. 36-51)

36. "Max is rushing in the morning's bagels to a restaurant on Second Avenue for the morning trade," c. 1940

37. "Cafeteria on East Broadway," September 12, 1941
*Orthodox Jews heard President Roosevelt on radio in East Side spots, like this restaurant at East Broadway and Jefferson Street. Their reaction, like that of other Americans, was quiet understanding, no excitement.* PM Photo by Weegee.

38. "Invitation to the dance," Rehearsal, Yiddish Theater, September 30, 1945

*Rehearsal at the Yiddish Art Theater, Second Avenue at Fourth Street, for the "Three Gifts," which opened October 1, 1945.* PM Photo by Weegee.

39. *The janitor takes time out to watch the rehearsal at the Yiddish Theater*, September 30, 1945. PM Photo by Weegee

40. "A taste of home," Greek Restaurant, July 1943
*Friends gather outside the neighborhood Greek café for the sounds of and news from friends back home.* New York Mirror.

40. *Caffé Bella Napoli*, Little Italy, July 1944.
*In Little Italy friends meet at the Café to exchange gossip and hear the latest news of the war in Italy.* New York Mirror.

41. *Tea break at the Café Royal on Second Avenue, meeting place for Yiddish Theater actors*, September 30, 1945

42. *Doyer Street Mission*, January 21, 1941
*Hard wooden benches fill a small auditorium, old newspapers cover. ...* PM Photo by Weegee.

43. *U.S. Hotel at 263 Bowery*, c. 1944

44. "The Bowery, in all night mission, men sit on benches, ... some thinking," December 26, 1940. PM Photo by Weegee.

45. *A man without legs and his cat*, c. 1939

45. *Drunken men in the Bowery*, c. 1943

46. *Heat spell*, May 23, 1941
*The hot weather last night took Weegee, the photographer, to the Lower East Side, where he found these children sleeping on a tenement fire escape at Irving and Rivington Streets. Weegee says he gave the kids $2 for ice cream. But their father took charge of the dough.* PM Photo by Weegee.

47. *Tenement sleeping*, June 1943
*Outdoor tenement sleepers at East Houston and Margin Streets....*

47. *Sleeping on the Fire Escape*, c. 1939
"... It's not so bad sleeping that way ... except when it starts to rain. ..." *Naked City*.

48. *Summer, the Lower East Side*, c. 1937

49. *Welcome Home, Jimmy*, July 12, 1943
*Jimmy Di Maggio, 3, missing 8 days, was found in Automat. Jimmy was kidnapped from a playground across the street from his home at 35 E. First St. The street before the Di Maggio home filled with a rejoicing crowd of more than 500 when the news was received.* PM Photo by Weegee.

50. *V-J Day Rally in Little Italy*, September 2, 1945
*Bonfire in Little Italy celebrating 'V-J Day.'* PM Photo by Weegee.

51. *The Juggler*, Lower East Side, July 1940
*Joe McWilliams, fascist-type candidate of the American Destiny Party, running for Congressman, is shown juggling eggs on Rivington Street.* PM Photo by Weegee.

## POLICE (pp. 52-67)

52-53. *Gunman Killed by Off Duty Cop at 344 Broome St.*, February 3, 1942
*Off Duty Cop Does Duty, Kills Gunman Who Tries Stickup. The boys were playing a little pool and cards in the Spring Arrow Social and Athletic Club, 344 Broome St., near the Bowery last night. Patrolman Eligio Sarro, off duty, went in for a pack of cigarets [sic]. Four men entered. "This is a stick-up," the leader muttered. Sarro was a little slow getting his hands out of his overcoat pockets. "Get 'em up," ordered the leader. Sarro did. One hand held a gun. When he got done firing, the leader was dead.* PM Photo by Weegee.

54. "Murder on the Roof," August 14, 1941
*Joseph Gallichio, 28, kept a candy store in the Bronx. In his spare time he raised racing pigeons. Last night, on the roof of 12 E. 106 St., he was murdered beside his pigeon cote. Five bullets entered his body. Police say he once sold narcotics. Neighbors watch from another roof while detectives take fingerprints of the dead man.* PM Photo by Weegee.

55. "Corpse with Revolver," August 7, 1936
*The body of Dominick Didato, who called himself Terry Burns, is shown where he was shot down in front of a restaurant at 90 Elizabeth Street. The fourth gangster to die within two weeks. Didato's death resulted, police say, from his attempts to break into Lucky Luciano's racket.* New York Post.

56. "On the Spot," c. 1940
"Slum Clearance Project, Hell's Kitchen."
*Murder victim lies on sidewalk in front of the Spot Bar and Grill at 10th Ave. and W. 46th St.*

57. "Rocco Finds His Pal Stabbed," July 31, 1941
"Who Done That?"
*A huge Great Dane dog was circling the body on the floor, not letting anyone near it. The owner of the place told me the dead man, Luigi Rivieccio, and the dog had been great friends. The dog had been outside and came in just after the fight to find his pal dead. Finally the cops formed a circle around the body and edged the dog out into the street.* PM Story and Photo by Weegee.

57. *Auto accident victim*, 1938
*An unidentified body, outlined with chalk, lies covered by a blanket, on sidewalk in front of a bar and grill.* New York Mirror.

58. "This was a friendly game of Bocci," c. 1939
*An argument started and one of the players was shot and killed. ...Naked City*.

59. "One-way Ride," 1940
*The body of unidentified murder victim lies on the sidewalk near the baby carriage.* New York Daily News.

60. *Bandit*, August 11, 1941
*Roy Bennett, 27, was slain by detectives when he tried to escape after attempting to hold up the New York Delicatessen, 1288 Sixth Ave. He had arrived from Texas by bus a few hours earlier, apparently planning to try his hand as big-city desperado.* PM Photo by Weegee.

61. "Joy of Living," April 17, 1942
*Car Hits 3d Ave. L — One Dies, Two Hurt. Under double-bill movie marquee, body of Stanley Stanley, was covered with newspapers and coats by police. Technical charge of homicide was lodged against Frank Whalen, who was taken*

to Bellevue Hospital for observation. Another passenger, Joseph Mahoney, also was hurt. PM Photo by Weegee.

62. "Murder in Hell's Kitchen," c. 1940
"One looks out of the windows…talks about the weather with a neighbor…or looks at murder." Naked City.

63. Murder at the Feast of San Gennaro, September 22, 1939
119 Mulberry Street, in the heart of Little Italy — during the early morning hours, Joseph (Little Joe) La Cava, 38, was slain, and Rocco (Chickee) Fagio, 40, was stabbed and shot by the gang. New York Mirror.

64-65. "Their First Murder," October 9, 1941
Pupils were leaving P.S. 143, in the Williamsburg section of Brooklyn, at 3:15 yesterday when Peter Mancuso, 22, described by police as a small-time gambler, pulled up in a 1931 Ford at a traffic light a block from the school. Up to the car stepped a waiting gunman, who fired twice and escaped through the throng of children. Mancuso, shot through the head and heart, struggled to the running board and collapsed dead on the pavement. The older woman is Mancuso's aunt, who lives in the neighborhood, and the boy, tugging at the hair of the girl in front of him, is her son, hurrying her away. PM Photo by Weegee.

65. "Here he is as he was left in the gutter…He's got a DOA tied to his arm, that means 'Dead on Arrival'," c. 1941. Naked City.

66. Manuelda Hernandez holds Manuel Jiminez in Her Lap, July 30, 1941
Weegee Covers: a Waterfront Shooting. Manuel Jiminez lies wounded in the lap of Manuelda Hernandez, in the El Mundo Restaurant on West Street at W. 12th St. He had been shot by Manuel Tribino, in an argument over Hernandez. She was crying. Police tried to lift Jiminez onto a stretcher, but Hernandez wouldn't let go of him. PM Story and Photo by Weegee.

67. Victim of Auto Accident Waiting for Doctor, September 25, 1940
"In Crash"
Jean Sledziski, 17, lies moaning on steps of a tenement house, after car in which she was riding crashed into an El pillar on First Ave., between 10th and 11th Sts. She suffered a fractured skull. Three others were hurt. All were taken to Bellevue Hospital. New York Daily News Photo by Weegee.

WEEGEE AND FILM NOIR Alain Bergala (pp. 68-77)

68. Photographer unknown. Weegee with poster for the film, The Naked City, c. 1948

71. "Police End Kids' Street Shower – Under Orders," August 18, 1944
At the corner of Cherry St. and Rutgers Pl. on the Lower East Side, sweltering kids turned on a fire hydrant and had a cooling shower until the cops came around. Under orders, the police turned the water off. In sympathy with the kids, however, they scolded no one and left at once to do the same job at the next corner. We suspect this hydrant went on again soon after the cops left. PM Photo by Weegee.

74. Accident victim under 3rd Ave. elevated train, 1939 New York World Telegram.

POLICE, cont. (pp. 78-117)

78. William Morey, Husband of Woman Who Killed Children and Herself, August 28, 1941
Tragedy in Brooklyn: Mother Kills Three Children and Herself. At 6:20 yesterday morning William Morey of 311 20th Street, Brooklyn, yelled for help. Morey was out Tuesday night and came home about 1:30 a.m. Stunned by a crack on the head, he came to in time to see his wife slit her throat. PM Photo by Weegee.

79. John Pulko, Accused Attacker Nabbed in Pistol Chase, September 18, 1939
John Pulko, of the Mills Hotel at 36th St. and Seventh Ave., a middle-aged peddler and war veteran, identified by a Washington Heights matron as the burglar who had criminally assaulted her at the point of a knife, was arrested by two radio patrolmen at 5 a.m. yesterday after a wild chase in which five shots were fired. New York Daily News Photo by Weegee.

80-81. Anthony Esposito, Accused "Cop Killer," January 16, 1941
Gunman Doesn't Want His Picture Taken. For the first time since Bruno Richard Hauptman, police today permitted photographers in the line-up room at headquarters. The subject was Anthony Esposito, under indictment with his brother, William, for the murder of a business man and a policeman in Tuesday's tragic Battle of Fifth Ave. The detectives, manacled to Esposito, didn't want their names or pictures in the papers. They obliged by turning around, holding the gunman by head and arm so he couldn't duck. The yardstick is on the line-up platform, where Esposito had stood, refusing to answer questions. "He looked like a sullen surly, snarling animal," Weegee reported. "He stumbled and sagged over to one side like a drunk." PM Story and Photo by Weegee.

82. Barber Confesses to Murder of Einer Sporrer, March 21, 1937
The barber, Salvatore Ossido, nervously dropped his scissors. Within 90 minutes after the discovery of the body, Ossido confessed. …Here he is being taken into the police station to be booked. A crowd of almost 1,000 shouted that Ossido should be lynched. New York Sunday Mirror.

83. After Vice Raid, January 18, 1941
Anna Swift's Girls Taken to Police Station. New York Mirror.

84. Henry Rosen (left) and Harvey Stemmer (center) were arrested for bribing basketball players, January 25, 1945. Henry Rosen (left) and Harvey Stemmer, alleged fixers in the Brooklyn College basketball scandal, cover up at Manhattan Police Headquarters. PM Photo by Weegee.

85. Frank Pape, Arrested for Homicide, November 10, 1944
Frank Pape, 16, a freshman at Bronx Vocational High School, is under arrest on a homicide charge. Police say he confessed tying up William Drach, 4, on Oct. 29, in the basement of 825 Eagle Ave., Bronx, after having seen it done in a movie. William strangled to death. The solution exonerates William's 8-year-old brother, Robert. PM Photo by Weegee.

86. Harold Horn, Knocked Over Milk Wagon with Stolen Car, June 27, 1941
Street Scene in New York: A Wild Kid in a Stolen Car Knocks Over Milk Wagon. Harold Horn, 16, already in trouble with the police, stole a car from a parking lot at 10th Ave. and 26th St. He tried to squeeze the car

between a milk wagon and a truck. The wagon was upset, the driver seriously hurt, and the car smashed against a light pole. A detective gets the captured driver into a police car and handcuffs him. PM Photo by Weegee.

87. Irma Twiss Epstein, Nurse Accused of Killing a Baby, February 9, 1942
Her face pale with grief, Nurse Irma Twiss Epstein, whose own baby died a year and a half ago, is booked at Morrisania Police Station in the death of a new-born baby whose crying was "driving me crazy." New York Daily News Photo.

88. "These are men arrested for dressing as girls…the cops, the old meanies broke up their dance…and took them to the pokey," c. 1939

89. "This boy was arrested for dressing like a girl," c. 1939

90-91. "The Gay Deceiver," c. 1939

91. "Meet Myrtle From Myrtle Ave.," November 26, 1943
Thomas Gill, 25, 160 57th St., Brooklyn, has a record of four arrests for burglary and petty larceny. Investigating at the station, the police found that Gill's feminine costume was complete… but that under the dress he wore a pair of rolled-up Army trousers. When asked to explain his attire, Gill said: "Well, you know, it was Thanksgiving, so I decided to masquerade as a woman." New York Post.

92. Major Green, Arrested for Murder, January 15, 1937. 6:15 A.M. Major Green, the slayer of Mrs. Mary Harriet Case, Jackson Heights bride, is booked at police station, Broadway and Justice Ave., Queens, following confession at 3:45 A.M. New York Daily News Photo.

93. Wife of Major Green being escorted out of police station, January 15, 1937. New York Daily News Photo.

94. Unidentified man in handcuffs at police station, c. 1941

95. "The lineup," 1939
Here is where the witnesses 'finger' the crooks, the murderers, the vandals. …New York Daily News.

96. "After the Street Fight…" c. 1940
"The best fights in town are on the sidewalks… and they are free for the spectators to enjoy… that is till a cop arrives to break it up… but the cops always arrive when the fights are over. This was a little argument outside Madison Square Garden. It was a much better fight than one sees on Friday nights.…I don't know what they were fighting about but I guess it was nothing trivial." Naked City.

97. "A New LOW in Arrests — Midget Seller of French Post Cards Arrested," April 18, 1940
Midget Fotog, Showman Held on Vice Charge. Jerry Austin was one of 10 members of alleged vice ring accused of forcing high school girls into prostitution. The pint-sized photographer, who operates a studio at 145 W. 45th St., was held on a rape charge. New York Daily News Photo.

98. "Factory Frankie" Aherns (left) and Marty Powell (right) Arrested for Association, February 17, 1937
Arrested on a charge for criminal association, "Factory Frankie" Ahern (left), racket pal of the late Dutch Schultz, and Marty Powell (right). New York Post.

99. *Charles Sodokoff and Arthur Webber Use Their Top Hats to Hide Their Faces*, January 27, 1942
*In Top Hats – In Trouble, Charles Sodokoff, 28, and Arthur Webber, 32, both Brooklynites, use their toppled toppers to hide faces as they take free ride to Felony Court. Boys were tippling at Astor Bar Saturday night when they decided to slide down banisters for fun (? ? ?). Cop was called and they assaulted him. Funsters then went from mahogany bar to iron type.* New York Daily News Photo.

100. *Man Caught in Store*, February 17, 1941
*Called early yesterday to investigate a broken candy store front window at 459 Broadway, just two blocks from Police Headquarters, detectives — and our police photographer, Weegee — arrived in time to meet this unnamed man coming out.* PM Photo by Weegee.

101. *Man Caught in Store, Led Away to Radio Car*, February 17, 1941
*Led away to a radio car, which took him to station house where he was booked on charges of burglary, the unnamed man calmly asked his captors for a light.* PM Photo by Weegee.

102. *Two Passengers Are Killed As Auto Dives Into Hudson*, January 25, 1942
*Police raise Connecticut auto that plunged into the Hudson at 29th St., on Saturday. Two people (one in car window) were killed....* PM Photo by Weegee.

103. *Ambulance Plunges Bringing Death to Two*, August 24, 1943
*A few hours after the Reception Hospital ambulance he was driving toppled into the East River, the body of Morris Linker is taken from the water. Swerving to avoid striking a pedestrian on Welfare Island, Linker lost control of the car and it struck an elderly patient, who later died.* PM Photo by Weegee.

104. *Cab Crash*, c. 1941
*A cab and a truck, tangled at 39th St. and 2nd Ave.*

105. *Car Crash Upper Fifth Ave.*, July 13, 1941
*4 a.m.: The street lights were turned out... two cars crashed. A badly cut-up youngster asks for a cigaret [sic] until the ambulance arrives. Weegee says cops resent accidents that happen around quitting time. Making out reports means overtime, no pay.* PM Photo by Weegee.

106. "*Death Strikes a Truck Driver at Dawn*," September 7, 1944
*Rudolph Supik, 38, 417 E. 10th St., the victim, lies dead in the street, the rolls and bread he was transporting shown near him.* PM Photo by Weegee.

107. "*...And the Living Suffer*," September 7, 1944
*Summoned by police to identify the victim, Mrs. Vanta Supik, his wife took one look, became hysterical. A couple of policemen helped her from the scene of the tragedy.* PM Photo by Weegee.

107. "*Sudden Death for One...Sudden Shock for the Other*," September 7, 1944
*Mrs. Dorothy Reportella, said by police to be the driver of the car which hit Supik's truck, still at the wheel of her sedan just after the crash. Shocked and hysterical, she was taken to Bellevue.* PM Photo by Weegee.

109. *Victim of Auto Accident*, October 29, 1939
*Here is another accident victim of the West Side Highway.*

*This crash near 12th St. left 1 dead and 2 injured.* New York Daily News.

110. "*Out of the River*," February 24, 1942
*At 9 last night, the car, a shiny black Buick, with Rhode Island license plates, was hoisted out of the river by a tug. Body of a Negro (feet are visible) was found in the car. Police Sgt. William Wilson eyewitnessed accident.* PM Photo by Weegee.

111. *Accident on Grand Central Station Roof*, 1944
*This car really took a 'wrong turn' off Park Ave. Car jumped the railing and almost went off the roof. Police are seen surveying the situation at 42nd St. and Vanderbilt Ave.* New York Mirror.

112-113. "*The dead lay still...*" August 18, 1941
*Three Women Trampled to Death in Excursion-Ship Stampede. When police had calmed the crowds crashing into the barriers in their haste to get aboard the excursion ship, the picnickers began to realize that scores must have been killed or injured. When this member of the lodge saw the blanket-covered bodies, he took his luncheon, his thermos bottle and left for home.* PM Photo by Weegee.

113. "*The Human Cop*," c. 1943

114. *Frank Birskowsky, on Sidewalk of the Bowery*, December 28, 1942
*To show one phase of Christmas on the Bowery, our photographer Weegee, snapped a picture of a man on the sidewalk of the Bowery near street number 269. Frank Birskowsky, 65, is pictured on sidewalk.* PM Photo by Weegee.

114. "*Hit by Taxi*," December 28, 1942
*Weegee walked on to the next block, heard commotion behind. Returning he found the man, attempting to cross the street, had been struck by a taxi.* PM Photo by Weegee.

114. "*Last Rites*," December 28, 1942
*Father Joseph L. Melody, Holy Name Mission, Bowery, administered last rites.* PM Photo by Weegee.

115. "*Comforted by Police*," December 28, 1942
*Birskowsky, taken to Bellevue Hospital, is expected to recover.* PM Photo by Weegee.

116. "*Night Duty*," July 20, 1941
*Two patrolmen dived into the Hudson after Donna Landon, 150 W. 47th St., who toppled in. They kept her afloat until a radio car and a New York Central tug brought help.* PM Photo by Weegee.

116. *Bringing Home the Bird*, December 1943
*"A truck loaded with 44 crates of chickens, 660 in total, driven by Irving Meinster, Woodridge, NY, collided at the intersection of 34th St. and Madison Ave. The driver of the other machine [was] Vito Lanza, 30-19 38th St., Long Island City. Chickens were everywhere. Firemen, taxi drivers, radio cars and the police emergency truck joined the hunt. There were 38 chickens missing after the chase...."* PM Story by Weegee.

117. *This Young Boy Got His Hand Caught in the Cup Machine*, c. 1942
*"Dead End Kid! This young boy, got his hand caught in the cup machine at the movie theatre, after his hand was gotten out he went back to see the show."*

FIRE (pp. 118-129)

118. "*Simply Add Boiling Water*," 1937
*The sign across the center of the building refers to the frankfurters, not the firemen. The American Kitchen Products building, at Water St., was extensively damaged.* Minicam Photography, July 1937

119. *Man covering face from smoke*, c. 1943

120. "*A couple driven out from the burning tenement...*," April 23, 1944
*Fire Alarm: Weegee calls this his favorite photo. It was made at dawn recently on Manhattan's Lower East Side during a tenement house fire. "The couple on the sidewalk," Weegee told us, "are watching the fire and hoping their belongings will not be burned. That is, the ones which the man had to leave behind."* PM Photo by Weegee.

121. "*I Cried When I Took This Picture.*" *Mrs. Henrietta Torres and Her Daughter Ada watch as Another Daughter and Her Son Die in Fire*, December 15, 1939
*"Mrs. Henrietta Torres and her daughter Ada, cry and look up hopelessly as another daughter and grandson were burned to death in the top floor of the tenement house at 41 Bartlett St., Brooklyn. Firemen couldn't reach them in time... on account of the stairway collapsing."* New York Daily News

122. "*What to Wear*," October 15, 1941
*What to wear at a fire is charmingly displayed by Morris Weinstock, who was in bed when he smelled smoke coming from the apartment below him at 130 Baruch Pl., Brooklyn. He ran down like this and warned the people in the burning flat. Everyone got out safely in night clothing.* PM Photo by Weegee.

123. *Elderly Woman Rescued from Fire at 209 West 62nd St.*, July 20, 1940
*An elderly woman goes down ladder, while fireman, behind and below her, helps her descend. Six firemen were overcome fighting this blaze, which caused considerable damage to the apartment house at 209 West 62nd St.* New York Daily News Foto by Fellig.

124. *Two-Alarm Blaze that Knocked Out 36 Firemen*, September 2, 1941
*Weegee Covers Two-Alarm Blaze that Knocked Out 36 Firemen. Firemen were called to 50th St. and Lexington Ave. to a basement fire in Steinbrook Pharmacy. They smashed their way into the store, but the heavy smoke was loaded with chemical gas and 36 firemen were overcome. One doctor devoted himself to administering soothing treatment to firemen whose throats were irritated by smoke. Many firemen had a much tougher time and artificial respirators were busy all night. A clerk locking up for the night, discovered the blaze.* PM Photo by Weegee.

125. *Ten Firemen Overcome in Washington Street Market Blaze*, May 19, 1941
*10 firemen were overcome while fighting a smoky blaze in the heart of Washington Market early today. The fire started in the basement of a three-story building occupied by Kraemer & Klie, banana dealers at 373 Washington St. The firemen had a tough enough time getting their apparatus past the numerous trucks and drays that clog the market. But when they got into the cellar, they dropped like flies as 400 crates of bananas, wrapped in wet straw and burlap, threw off carbon monoxide. All the firemen were revived.* PM Photo by Weegee.

126. "Two Firemen Rescuing Angel," 1939
*Firemen get to rescue people, cats up trees, loose chickens, … and as in this picture an Angel too.* New York World Telegram Photo.

127. "Someone rushed in and saved the Holy Scrolls from the Synagogue," March 2, 1943
*Fire swept the five-story loft building at 372 E. Houston St., Manhattan. Some small manufacturing firms and the Congregation Israel Anscheigal Icie Minhagsford occupy the building. Holy Scrolls were carried out by members of the congregation.* PM Photo by Weegee.

128. *Fire Lieutenant Vincent Burns rescues Mrs. Carl Taylor from a Fire at 136 W. 64th St.,* January 13, 1941
*Fire Lieutenant Rescues Woman From Fourth Floor of Burning Building. This is how Weegee got the picture: "I was covering a two-alarm auto showroom fire on Broadway. Suddenly I heard sirens. I ran to the corner and saw engines turning west into 64th St. I saw smoke coming out of a house in the middle of the block. On the fourth floor a woman was screaming at the window as a fireman held on to her to keep her from jumping. Before the aerial ladder could be raised Fire Lieutenant Vincent Burns ran in and carried out the hysterical woman. A police man took her away. She was Mrs. Carl Taylor, 51, of 136 W. 64th St."* PM Photo by Weegee.

128. *Henry Geller, Weeps Over Loss of His Tobacco Shop,* July 28, 1941
*East Side Fire: Landlord Weeps as Porter Burns to Death. Henry Geller, landlord at 312 E. Houston St., weeps over the loss of his tobacco shop on the first floor.* PM Photo by Weegee.

129. *Brooklyn Mattress Factory Burned,* February 1, 1942
*When Brooklyn mattress factory burned yesterday at 249 Willoughby St., opposite Raymond St. jail, three alarms were turned in.* PM Photo by Weegee.

**SAMMY'S** (pp. 130-139)

130-131. *Norma Devine is Sammy's Mae West,* December 4, 1944

131. "Sammy's on the Bowery," December, 1944.
"Among the flop houses and missions you'll find Sammy's Bowery Follies, No. 267 on the Bowery, 'the poor man's Stork Club.' It is a haven for derelicts and a hangout for the well heeled. Entertainment is provided by not only the 'past-their-prime' vaudevillians, but also by the frowzy men and blowzy women." *LIFE.*

132. *Tilly Schneider – songs sweet and low,* December 4, 1944

133. *Monty Reed, "Master of Ceremonies,"* December 4, 1944

133. *Daisy Lewis, Entertainer,* January 16, 1944

134. *Billie Dausha (left) and Mabel Sidney (right), Bowery Entertainers,* December 4, 1944

135. "The Bowery Saving's Bank," December 4, 1944

136. "After the Opera… at Sammy's Night Club on the Bowery," c. 1944

136. "Blond woman, after the Opera… at Sammy's Night Club on the Bowery," c. 1944

137. "Sophisticated Lady," c. 1943

137. "Sammy and Guests," c. 1943

138. "New Year's at 5 in the morning in a night club, I found this 3 year old with his parents welcoming in the New Year with milk," 1943.

138. *Hot dog vendor at Sammy's Bar,* c. 1943. *Naked City.*

139. "Shorty, the Bowery Cherub, New Year's Eve at Sammy's Bar," 1943. *Naked City.*

**CONEY ISLAND** (pp. 140-147)

140-141. "Crowd at Coney Island, Temperature 89 degrees… They came early, and stayed late," July 22, 1940
*Weegee, whose real name is Arthur Fellig, took this picture at four in the afternoon. The temperature was 89 degrees. The Coney Island Chamber of Commerce guessed there were 1,000,000 people. Nobody really knows.* PM Photo by Weegee.

141. *First Aid for Ripped Slacks,* June 9, 1941. "A Stitch in Time."
"I don't know how Mama happened to bring along a needle and thread, but I didn't pose the picture. You don't have to do that to get amusing pictures at Coney. I go out every summer to photograph the crowds. They're always the same and always different. One difference from 1910 and yesterday was the number of soldiers in uniform on boardwalk, looking over the gals on the sand." PM Story and Pictures by Weegee.

141. *During the War,* c. 1944
*Listening to the baseball game, at the beach, was a cheap way of spending the afternoon.* PM Photo by Weegee.

142. "Lovers at Coney Island," c. 1943
[Infrared Negative]

143. "Girl on Life Guard Station," c. 1940
[Infrared Negative]
"I walked nearer to the water's edge and stopped to rest against a Life Guard Station look-out. I thought I heard a movement from above so I aimed my camera high and took a photo, thinking it was a couple who liked to be exclusive and do their love making nearer the sky. When I developed the picture, I saw that the only occupant on the look-out had been a girl looking dreamily towards the Atlantic Ocean." *Naked City.*

143. "Lovers on the Sand," c. 1943
[Infrared Negative]
"Once in a while I would hear a giggle or a happy laugh, so I aimed my camera and took a picture in the dark using invisible light." *Naked City.*

144. *Sunbathing,* January 20, 1941
*This was the only sunbather Weegee found yesterday at Coney Island. He sits in front of a padlocked shooting gallery near boardwalk.* PM Photo by Weegee.

145. "Lost Children," June 9, 1941
"I had been waiting three hours to get a picture of the official first lost child of the new season when a man came over to the Park Department attendant with this boy and said, 'Lost child.' Pretty soon his wild-eyed mother came up and took him away. The child was making such a rumpus, and the mother seemed so excited about it all, that I didn't want to bother them to ask their names and address." PM Story and Photo by Weegee.

146. *Spring Sunbathers,* March 24, 1941
*Some people like the beach when there isn't a crowd.* PM Photo by Weegee.

147. *Spring Comes to Coney Island,* March 24, 1941
*Here's… the crowd at 3 p.m. yesterday, first Sunday of Spring. Sunday sunners in overcoats at Coney. On beach, a few in bathing suits. Mercury stood at 52 when Weegee took picture.* PM Story and Photo by Weegee.

**PICTURING NEW YORK, THE NAKED CITY**
Ellen Handy (pp. 148-159)

149. *Striking Beauty,* July 29, 1940
*This remarkable foto [sic] shows a bolt of lightning apparently striking City Bank Farmer's Trust Co., at 20 Exchange Place, during Saturday night's storm. The fotog shot foto on South St., near Brooklyn Bridge.* New York Daily News Foto by Arthur Fellig.

150. "Check for Two Murders," c. 1939

151. Paul Strand, *Blind Woman,* New York, 1916. Photogravure from *Camera Work,* nos. XLIX-L, June 1917, Permanent Collection, International Center of Photography, New York.

156. Alfred Stieglitz: *The Terminal,* c. 1892-3 Photogravure from *Camera Work,* no. 36, October, 1911, Permanent Collection, International Center of Photography, New York.

156. *Incident in the Snowstorm,* December 28, 1944
*Sam Karshnowitz, a rag peddler, rented a horse from a stable for the day to pull his wagon. The horse slipped in the snow last night at 14th St. and Fifth Ave. Bystanders helped Karshnowitz get the horse on its feet again, and the two went on about their business.* PM Photo by Weegee.

**TIMES SQUARE** (pp. 160-169)

160. "Ten Cents a Dance," Roseland, Times Square, c. 1943
"Okay it's your dime…" *Naked City.*

161. "Dancing Tonite," New Gardens, Times Square, c. 1944

162. *This woman is concerned about the D-Day Invasion,* June 7, 1944

163. *Woman looking at electric sign on the New York Times Building,* June 7, 1944

163. "The Faces of New York on Invasion Day," June 6, 1944

164. "A Trip to Mars," Times Square, c. 1943

165. *Viewing News Report of Yankee Game,* October 6, 1943
*This is how New York received news from Yankee Stadium yesterday afternoon. PM's photographer took the picture through a window as the passing crowd watched the score board in the upper window of the Sachs Furniture Co. Store.* PM Photo by Weegee.

166. *Macy's Santa*, November 21, 1940
*Inflation of Santa Claus for Macy's parade required two hours, 12 men, 8000 cubic feet of helium gas, 150 feet of protecting canvas, a vacuum cleaner … PM Photo by Weegee.*

167. *Macy's Parade – Clown and Crew*, c. 1942

167. *Woman Cab Driver and Macy's Clown*, c. 1942
*"Don't be SCARED… LADY CAB DRIVER… cruising down COLUMBUS AVE in the rain… it's just the hand of a 45 FT. CLOWN being filled with HELIUM GAS for the annual MACYS DEPARTMENT STORE Thanksgiving parade…" Weegee's People.*

168. *Acrobat goes Head over Heels…* , c. 1943

169. *"Radio City Music Hall Actor… ,"* c. 1944
*Even geese like to send postcards to friends. This one is a member of the Radio City Music Hall Revue. PM Photo by Weegee.*

### THE OPERA (pp. 170-179)

170. *"The Opera Opened Last Night,"* December 3, 1940

171. *"The Socialites,"* c. 1941

172. *The Fashionable People* [ title first used for "The Critic" in *LIFE* magazine, December 6, 1943]
*…were laden with jewels. Most bejeweled were Mrs. George W. Kavanaugh and Lady Decies whose entry was viewed with distaste by a spectator. LIFE.*

173. *In the Lobby at the Metropolitan Opera, Opening Night*, November 22, 1943

174. *Metropolitan Opera's Women's Chorus Rehearsal*, November 26, 1944

175. *Metropolitan Opera's Men's Chorus Rehearsal*, November 26, 1944
*Members rehearse their parts as knights, for Wagner's Lohengrin. PM Photo by Weegee.*

176. *Champagne in ice bucket*, c. 1941

176. *Opening Night, Metropolitan Opera*, c. 1943
[Infrared Negative]
177. *Woman at Metropolitan Opera*, c. 1943
[Infrared Negative]
*"I don't know if he's admiring her shoulder, or is going to take a bite."*

177. *Intermission, Metropolitan Opera*, c. 1943
[Infrared Negative]

178. *"Louella Parsons at the Opera,"* c. 1945

179. *"Opening Night at the 'Met,'"* December 3, 1944
[Infrared Negative]
*"Monday evening – during the first act of Faust – the photographer used infra-red film and invisible light to get this striking study of listeners in the back part of the orchestra. Infra-red heavies up some beards." PM Photo by Weegee.*

### WAR (pp. 180-189)

180. *"Down With The Japs The Rats,"* October 18, 1942
*Small Fry on Lower East Side Honor Big Brothers in the Services. Six-year-old Joseph Luparelli, wearing his brother's Army coat and cap, was in the crowd that turned out last Sunday.… PM Photo by Weegee.*

181. *"A Time of Great Optimism, and Lingering Doubt,"* May 7, 1945
*An air-raid warden in Times Square walked his baby back home.… New York Times Magazine.*

182. *Subway Station serves as Blackout Shelter*, August 13, 1943
*When all subway power was cut off at 5:38 p.m., this Brooklyn bound crowd gathered on the platform at Canal and Lafayette Sts. "Conditions were quiet and orderly,…" PM Photo by Weegee.*

183. *V-J Day Victory Parade in Little Italy*, September 6, 1945

184. *Young East Siders Hang Hirohito in Effigy…*, October 11, 1942

185. *"Time is Short"* March 23, 1942
*Little Italy held another Service Raising Rally yesterday. PM Photo by Weegee.*

186. *Parades are so tiring…*, c. 1943

187. *Celebration at End of War*, c. 1945

188. *"Der Fuehrer's Birthday,"* April 21, 1942
*Times Sq. Last Night looked like this as New York's first big war rally was held to dramatize Government's War Stamps and Bond drive. Special police detail handled crowds. Hitler (it was his birthday) was hanged in effigy. John Garfield, actor, read editorial This is the Year by Ralph Ingersoll from yesterday's PM. Bonds were sold at street side booths, while girls in the crowd sold stamps. PM Photo by Weegee.*

189. *"TIMES SQUARE – early Tuesday morning,"* August 1945

189. *"There was Dancing in the Streets of New York,"* May 1945
*"UNCONDITIONAL SURRENDER OF THE WEHRMACHT, Although Still Unofficial, was cue for a bunch of youngsters to carry over their celebrating far into the evening on Times Square. They brought along their musical instruments, sat on cars and sent a solid number bouncing down the WHITE WAY. 2 sailors caught the mood, and to the delight of bobby soxers who beat time with their hands, danced a modern, victory version of 'THE SIDEWALKS OF NEW YORK.'" PM Photo by Weegee.*

189. *"There were Hugs for Everyone,"* c. 1945

189. *"Celebrating V-J Day at the Times Square Statue of Liberty,"* September 6, 1945

### LOVERS (pp. 190-193)

190. *On top of the Empire State Building*, c. 1942

191. *After midnight in Washington Square, Folk Dance*, c. 1955

192. *"Scene I – the Warm-up,"* c. 1948

192. *"Scene II – the Kiss,"* c. 1948

192. *"Scene III — the Clutch,"* c. 1948

193. *"Alone in their dream,"* July 23, 1946
*"Young dancers forget the music, forget everyone but each other." Look.*

### HARLEM (pp. 194-203)

194. *"Easter Sunday in Harlem,"* April 26, 1943
*Easter paraders in Harlem made a fine showing with new suits and dresses. These girls were photographed as they left the Abyssinian Baptist Church. All Harlem churches were packed with worshippers. PM Photo by Weegee.*

195. *"Easter Sunday in Harlem,"* c. 1940
*"I spotted this happy man coming out of church… he told me that he was a clothing salesman… and that every Easter Sunday he puts on his full dress suit." Naked City.*

196. *"Calypso,"* c. 1944

197. *"She feels the BEAT… ,"* c. 1944

197. *"At the Jazz Concert,"* c. 1944

198-199. *Boys Caught in Boarded-up Harlem Store*, August 16, 1943
*Radio policemen caught these three teen-age boys inside a riot-wrecked drug store at 145th St. and Eighth Ave. The boys were taken to the 135th St. Station House with "loot" consisting of some nickel bags of Bull Durham smoking tobacco. PM Photo by Weegee.*

200. *"The Lottery Ticket,"* c. 1950

201. *"N.A.A.C.P.,"* c. 1943

202. *"She's got the SPIRIT,"* c. 1943

203. *"With a song in my heart,"* c. 1948

### ENTERTAINMENT (pp. 204-215)

204. *Vera Middleton, singer with Louie Armstrong*, c. 1948

205. *"At a Jazz Concert,"* c. 1948

205. *"Any Partner will do… ,"* c. 1948

206. *"This is a 'Frankie Fan,'"* October 12, 1944
*'Frankie fans' wear clothes like their idol, and bring him offerings of all shapes, sizes and origin.… PM Photo by Weegee.*

207. *Frank Sinatra*, Paramount Theater, October 12, 1944
*Frank Sinatra began an engagement at the Paramount Theater here yesterday. He reached the theater at 6 a.m. yesterday, but by that time, a long line – about 1000 kids, mostly bobby sox girls – had already been waiting for hours in the chill air of early morning. While they waited and the line grew longer, Sinatra rehearsed inside the empty theater with Raymond Paige and his orchestra. PM Photo by Weegee.*

207. "And a girl smiles too… Then she cries… The Swoon," November 5, 1944
*The followers of "The Voice" are not all girls. But it's the girls who really get "sent" when he sings. The Bobby Sox Brigade watched him enthralled – in an ecstacy belonging to another world. PM Photos by Weegee.*

208. "A phone booth is a handy place to make a date… ," c. 1944

209. "Dressing Room at a New Orleans 'Burly-Que,'" October 4, 1950

210. "Call Board," c. 1950

210. "Any bed will do… ," c. 1950

211. "Sonata in G-Strings," c. 1950

212. *Audience listening to Jazz band playing "Bell Bottom Trousers,"* c. 1944

213. *Woman Listening to Bunk Johnson Concert, Stuyvesant Casino,* c. 1944

213. *Women calling out at Jazz concert, Stuyvesant Casino,* c. 1944

214. "Whistler's Mother," Arts Ball, Waldorf Astoria Hotel, New York, c. 1948

215. *Masquerade Ball,* Waldorf Astoria Hotel, c. 1943

### MOVIE THEATERS (pp. 216-227)

216. *Audience in the Palace Theater,* c. 1950 [Infrared Negative]

217. "Couple at the Palace Theater," c. 1943 [Infrared Negative]

217. "Lovers at the Palace Theater," c. 1945 [Infrared Negative]

217. *Sailor and girl at the movie,* c. 1943 [Infrared Negative]

218. *Children,* Palace Theater, c. 1943 [Infrared Negative]

218. *Children,* Palace Theater, c. 1943 [Infrared Negative]

219. *Girls watching movie,* Palace Theater, c. 1943 [Infrared Negative]

220. "The show's over," c. 1943 [Infrared Negative]

221. *Girl eating popcorn in the movies,* c. 1943 [Infrared Negative]

222-223. *Girls laughing at movie,* c. 1943 [Infrared Negative]

224. *Woman sleeping in movie theater,* c. 1943 [Infrared Negative]

224. *Sleeping at the movies,* c. 1943 [Infrared Negative]

225. *Overhead view of theater sleeper,* c. 1943 [Infrared Negative]

226. "Lovers at the Palace Theater I," c. 1945 [Infrared Negative]

226. "Lovers at the Palace Theater II," c. 1945 [Infrared Negative]

226. "Lovers at the Palace Theater III," c. 1945 [Infrared Negative]

227. "Lovers at the Palace Theater," c. 1945 [Infrared Negative]

### THE CIRCUS (pp. 228-233)

228. "Tired Businessman at the Circus… ," June 28, 1943

229. *Resourceful girl manages to watch man on the flying trapeze and feed hot dog to escort at same time.* April 18, 1943. PM Photo by Weegee.

230. "Boom," June 28, 1943
*Miss Victory, Eglie Zacchini, is shot out of a cannon. PM Photo by Weegee.*

230. "Here she comes," June 28, 1943
*Here you see Miss Zacchini as she begins to 'shoot' from cannon. PM Photo by Weegee.*

230. "She's almost out," June 28, 1943
*Miss Zacchini, as she flies at a speed of 360 feet a second. PM Photo by Weegee.*

230. "Off she goes," June 28, 1943
*Weegee got these unusually difficult pictures at a performance using a telephoto lens at 1/1000th of a second. PM Photo by Weegee.*

231. *Boy at circus,* April 18, 1943. PM Photo by Weegee.

232. "Circus Elephant at Madison Square Garden," c. 1942

233. "Jimmy Armstrong, the Clown," c. 1943

### THE VILLAGE (pp. 234-237)

234. "Village Concert," c. 1951

235. "Blowing soap bubbles is fun, too…" Washington Square Park, c. 1944. *Weegee's People.*

236. "Girls at the Bar," c. 1946

237. "At San Ramo's," c. 1945

### PERSONALITIES (p. 239-247)

239. *Henry Fonda, Clark Gable and Bette Davis,* Hollywood, c. 1949

240. *Louie Armstrong, backstage at Basin Street,* New York, c. 1950

241. *Jimmy Durante surrounded by his young fans in Italian Restaurant,* Little Italy, c. 1948

242. "Stieglitz," May 7, 1944
*Alfred Stieglitz, "a great photographer," in the office of his gallery. PM Story and Photo by Weegee.*

243. "Lisette Model, at Nick's Jazz Joint," c. 1946

244. "Jerry Lewis and his friends," Hollywood, c. 1950

245. "Hopper's Topper," Hedda Hopper, Hollywood, c. 1948

246. *Jayne Mansfield,* Hollywood, c. 1951

247. "Peter Sellers, Stanley Kubrick, during filming of Dr. Strangelove," 1963

### DISTORTIONS (pp. 248-251)

248. *Jerry Lewis* (kaleidoscope), c.1956

248. *Zero Mostel – Samuel Joel* (kaleidoscope), c.1958

248. *The Rockettes* (kaleidoscope), c.1958

248. Untitled (photomontage of Dora Pelletier, from 1941— an entertainer at Sammy's-on-the-Bowery — inside a champagne bottle), c.1959

248. Untitled (photomontage of "Lovers," July 1946 inside a perfume bottle), c.1959

248. Untitled (photomontage of "Lovers" in Washington Square Park, Greenwich Village, c. 1946 inside a half-gallon bottle), c.1959

249. *Marilyn Monroe* (plastic lens), c.1960

249. *Talent Scout in "Naked Hollywood"* (self-portrait), c.1950-52

250. *Tate Gallery, London* (plastic lens), c.1960s

250. Untitled (night club musician from c.1946, plastic lens), c.1960

250. *London* (plastic lens), c.1960

251. *Weegee and Model* (mirror effect/double image), c.1953-56

251. *Nude* (mirror effect/double image), c.1953-56. "Weegee's Women," *Showplace* [First Edition] (July 1956).

251. *Nude* (plastic lens and patterned glass), c.1953-56. "Weegee's Women," *Showplace* [First Edition] (July 1956).

251. *Nude* (easel trick and plastic lens), c.1953-56, "Weegee's Women," *Showplace* [First Edition] (July 1956).